POVERTY ALLEVIATION STRATEGIES OF NGOs

About the Author

D. Rajasekhar is an Associate Professor (Economics) in Decentralisation and Development Unit of the Institute for Social and Economic Change, Bangalore. He is currently directing a World Bank supported research project on 'Roles of Rural Local Organisations in Development Projects', and a Karnataka Government supported project on 'Panchayat Finances in Karnataka'. His research interests include local organisations, micro-finance and linkages among the development actors. He recently published two books, *Rejuvenating Tanks : A Socio-Ecological Approach*, and *Decentralised Government and NGOs: Issues, Strategies and Ways Forward.*

Poverty Alleviation Strategies of NGOs

D. Rajasekhar
Decentralisation and Development Unit
Institute for Social and Economic Change, Bangalore

CONCEPT PUBLISHING COMPANY, NEW DELHI-110059

ISBN : 81-8069-090-3

First Published 2004

Published and Printed by
Ashok Kumar Mittal
Concept Publishing Company
A/15-16 Commercial Block, Mohan Garden
New Delhi-110059 (India)

Phones : 25351460, 25351794
Fax : 091-11-25357103
E-mail : publishing@conceptpub.com

Preface

The central hypothesis of the study is that while the poor must be central actors in any attempt to bring about a reduction in the poverty condition, the endogenous development of the poor by the poor is not possible. The structural nature of poverty and the structures and processes of development require that the actions of the poor be supported by those of the state and other agencies in order to secure the rights, and policies that can benefit the poor and secure their development. The emergence of NGOs as important development actors in India implies that one can hope for more attention from the development actors [line departments, Panchayati Raj Institutions (PRIs), etc.] to the needs and concerns of the poor in policy formulation and implementation.

In this study, the poverty alleviation strategies of NGOs, and other actors with the help of case study method have been analysed. Primary data were collected from six villages covered by two NGOs (SHARE in Vellore district in Tamil Nadu and Sanghamitra in Krishna District in Andhra Pradesh) through a questionnaire and PRA techniques. In two of the villages in each project area, the NGO was working, while in another it was not.

Condition and Severity of Poverty in the Selected Villages

The magnitude of poverty varied within and across the villages. In general, most of the poor households belonged to SC community. The severity of poverty also varied: in general, it was high among

SC households. Even among these households, the women bore the brunt of poverty. The principal causes of poverty were endowment (assets such as land) and exchange (unemployment) failures.

Poverty Alleviation Interventions by NGOs

The poverty alleviation interventions of the NGOs were in the form of undertaking economic programmes (craft activity) to provide employment, providing micro-finance services to enable the poor to access the credit for income generation and enabling the people to use the strength of the organisation (namely, SHGs) to obtain political and social empowerment.

The micro-finance and income generation programmes made a difference to the poor covered by the NGOs in so far as income, occupational diversification, acquisition of skills and confidence. However, this was not widespread. Societal constraints and lack of infrastructure at the village level prevented women from borrowing for income generation.

Another conclusion was that women's income formed a large proportion of the total household income. A majority of such households were headed by women and the contribution of male income was low (often due to illness, drinking). The evidence also suggests that enabling women to earn income might result in a situation of male members withdrawing from the labour market. This phenomenon put a lot of pressure on them. The implication of this finding is that men should also be brought within the purview of development intervention if women are to be empowered.

Years of membership in micro-finance groups has made only marginal difference in so far as the participation of women in the political institutions. The qualitative evidence on participation in political institutions indicates that the SHG membership had not really contributed to gaining awareness on rights that the women had and how to utilize these rights.

Poverty Alleviation Interventions by Local Organisations

The poverty alleviation programmes of line departments, PRIs, Banks, etc., had the potential to address the root causes of poverty, namely, lack of assets (land) and unemployment. But, the line department programmes were mainly related to the PDS, OAP and some bank loans. Banks did not provide credit for income generation or asset building. The programmes of gram panchayat were essentially related to building the infrastructure in the village, and they did not incorporate the concerns of the poor. Thus, there was no clear congruence between the situation of the poor and poverty alleviation programmes undertaken by the local organisations.

Poverty Alleviation Strategies of the People

The *mutah* (gang) labour, an important organising practice of agricultural labourers in Andhra villages, improved the bargaining position of the labourers, helped them in securing more employment and wages, maximising the family income by recruiting children and the old, and reducing the gender gap in wages. All these are well known infirmities of the agricultural labour market in India. The strong point of *mutah* labour is that it has succeeded in having a positive impact on these infirmities. These benefits have, at best, solved the livelihood problems of the poor. The *mutahs* labour does not help the labourers in acquiring resources, knowledge and assert their rights. This is, in part, due to the fact that the *mutahs* are not horizontally and vertically integrated into the decision-making and implementation channels. The local trade unions, government departments, banks and NGOs are very well aware of *niutahs;* but, does not realise their potential in poverty reduction. Hence, *mutahs* have been kept outside their policies and programme implementation.

Constraints and Obstacles Faced by the NGOs in Poverty Alleviation

The important causes of poverty were lack of assets and unemployment. The local organisations formed for them had only limited success in addressing these causes. The NGOs, which were supposed to have facilitated the mechanisms to enable the poor to represent their interests and secure them, also had limited success in this regard for the following reasons.

- The basis for the intervention strategy was not entirely rooted in the poverty condition and processes in the local area.
- The NGOs could not represent the interests of the poor in the policy and implementation channels because the mechanisms through which the poor households became well-off were largely individual and entrepreneur based strategies. This suggests that, historically it was not a socio-political process among the poor, which helped them to influence decision-making, agendas, policy and programme implementation at the local level so that they could secure their interests. This further implies that the collective memory of the poor was not one of social and political processes where they had influenced the policy and implementation issues in their favour.
- The institutional channels created by NGO were inadequate to help the poor to access, control and contest the policy formulation and implementation. The SHGs formed by the organisation were not homogeneous, and consisted of poorest, poor and others. Such heterogeneity often came in the way of generating and facilitating the possibilities for the poor to exert influence on political and economic process. In the meetings of the craft centre, members were pre-occupied with the production of palm-leaf products, and they only talked about orders, production, quality and meeting deadlines. The monthly meetings of SHGs were mainly utilised for savings collection and to arrive at lending decisions. Vety little time was spent on discussing issues relating to the community and to their poverty. Further, there was no forum either at the village or gram panchayat level where members of the SHGs and craft centres could come together to exert influence on political and economic processes. Similarly, the priority given to building or becoming part of NGO network to represent the interests of the poor in the policy formulation and implementation was low.
- The existence of poverty at the local level has been recognised and the poor themselves identify the causes

poverty. The political discourse of poverty at the local level probably stops here. The views on culpability for the condition of the poor and the emphasis on individual strategies suggested that the political discourse on poverty at the local level remains very broad and diffused. Very often, the discussion on who is responsible for poverty alleviation does not take place at the local level. The 'non-conduct of gram sabha meetings' is not discussed in group meetings because of the widespread perception that the mandate given to gram panchayats is not poverty reduction; but, something else. The work of PRIs relating to sanitation, protected water supply and road construction is all important for poverty alleviation. But, though gram panchayats can take up work relating to the desilting of tanks, improving the water table in the locality, providing sanitary facilities for women, undertaking employment oriented public works for the poor, etc., they were not on the agenda. The target group of NGOs did not make any efforts to take the discourse on poverty to the local organisations as they were unsure about who was responsible for their poverty reduction.

- The target group members of NGOs also could not obtain the support of the other poor in the villages because of exclusive practices adopted, and coverage of only a small proportion of the poor in a village. The work of NGOs on income generation and welfare might have helped its own target group but it failed to include the other poor to join in the endeavour to represent the interests of the poor in policy formulation and implementation.

To conclude, the NGOs have been making efforts to fulfil the objective of empowerment of poor women and implementing programmes and activities aimed at livelihood security and capacity building. They have been, however, facing constraints and obstacles in generating the possibilities for the poor to reduce their poverty. The constraints reflect deficiencies in their technical and political capacity. The obstacles are wider socio-economic and political processes and lack of pro-poor attitude among the other local organisations. Given that NGOs alone cannot reduce poverty and other local organisations are not pro-poor in their nature, poverty reduction remains to be an outstanding problem. This calls for linkages among the local organisations in assessing the situation of the people, and planning, implementation and monitoring of development programmes.

—**D. RAJASEKHAR**

Acknowledgements

This book is the outcome of a research project on 'Poverty Alleviation Strategies' undertaken at ADRT Unit in the Institute for Social and Economic Change, Bangalore, with financial support from GTZ, SHPAP, New Delhi. My heartfelt thanks are due to Ms. Gabrielle Ramm, Team Leader, GTZ, SHPAP, for entrusting this important work to the institute, and offering valuable suggestions, comments and criticisms at various stages of the work. I also thank Mrs. Namerta and her colleagues at SHF, Bangalore, for their help in organising the steering group meetings, and providing their own academic inputs and facilitating the provision of inputs from Ms. Ranjani Krishnamurthi and Mr. Nadarajan.

This study received liberal and willing support from Mr. Murugesan and his colleagues at SHARE, and Mrs. Vani and her colleagues at Saghamitra, the two NGOs selected for the study. I do hope that this study will be of some help in the attempts of SHARE and Sanghamitra at poverty alleviation and empowerment of the rural poor.

Some parts of the study were presented in three seminars and workshops. These were 'Political Space for Poverty Reduction', 'Organising Practices and Economic Control' (both organised by the Centre for Development Research at Copenhagen, Denmark) and 'Impact of Micro-Finance on Empowerment of Women' (organised at ISEC). I thank all the participants, especially Dr. Neil Webster, Dr. Lars-Enberg Pedersen, Dr. Ole Tekeldsen, Dr. Gita Sen and Prof. V.M. Rao for their comments on the draft chapters. I also thank Professors M. Govinda Rao and R.S. Deshpande for their support in completing the study.

Ms. P. Shobana, Mr. R.R. Biradar, Mr. Krishne Gowda, Ms. M. Shanthi, Ms. R. Manjula and Ms. Sujani provided excellent research support to the project.

Last but not least, the people in the selected villages enthusiastically participated in the PRA exercises, and shared their life experiences without any fear or favour. I do hope that this study will be used by the policy makers and other development actors in making 'things better for the poor'.

—**D. RAJASEKHAR**

Contents

1

Introduction

Growing numbers of the poor and alleviation of poverty have been the concerns of successive Indian governments since independence in 1947. The policy response to this concern can be seen in the shift from capital intensive growth-oriented strategies with assumptions of trickle-down effect in the 1960s and 1970s to launching of a nation-wide anti-poverty programmes in the late-1970s and 1980s. Since 1991, macro-policies aimed at growth with equity, linking the economy with global markets, reduced role for the state, privatisation of development [by involving the Non-Governmental Organisations (NGOs) in development work] and decentralisation in administration have been brought in. During the last five decades, a number of local organisations have been created, administration decentralised and space provided for the NGOs so that the macro-policies are implemented, the interests of the poor represented and a broad based development, poverty alleviation and reduction made possible. A positive impact of these developments is that the proportion of people living below the poverty line declined especially from 1970 onwards primarily due to agricultural growth; yet, the number of absolute poor have increased and those crossing the poverty line have become vulnerable.

In this context, the distinction between poverty alleviation and poverty reduction becomes very pertinent. Poverty alleviation is a short-term improvement of the poor's capital endowment. Poverty reduction is a long-term elimination of the poor's dependency on social relations, and of vulnerability with respect to changes in their environment (Pedersen and Webster 1998). Thus, while agricultural growth and better access to markets can alleviate poverty, the involvement of poor in the development efforts becomes crucial for poverty reduction. Further, "poverty reduction requires the generation and facilitation of opportunities for the poor and organisations working on their behalf to exert influence on political and economic processes" (Webster and Pedersen 2002). Poverty reduction also requires building of the capacity of the poor through the provision of knowledge and information so that they can identify the needs, articulate their rights, gain access to resources, and change the terms of engagement with other organisations. If NGOs are defined as those organisations which facilitate the implementation of development programmes for the poor, then they are the ones in India who can work on behalf of the poor, and generate and facilitate opportunities for the poor to exert influence on political and economic processes.

There is a widespread belief (and acceptance) in India that NGOs, by virtue of being small in scale, flexible, innovative, participatory, focusing on development and relatively independent, are more successful in reaching the poor and in poverty alleviation. This has contributed to the increasing popularity of the NGOs among the government and external aid agencies, and their rapid growth. Notwithstanding the charges of corruption and lack of accountability and public transparency on some of the NGOs, the last ten years has witnessed improved credibility and legitimacy for the NGOs.[1]

With the growing numbers and increased funding, the NGOs have been able to create a vast social infrastructure. It is estimated that there are 20,000 NGOs active in rural development today.[2] If we assume that each of these NGOs is working in 10 villages, the NGOs together will be covering half of the villages in India. If we assume that each of the NGOs has five trained workers, the number of qualified persons engaged in rural development will be large. A majority of the NGOs have formed people's organisations at the village level, provided education and training to the people on various issues, and most of them work with the marginalised groups such as women, *dalits* and *adivasis*. This social infrastructure provides ample opportunities for NGOs not only for making service provision but also to enable the poor to access the resources from the government, to enter into gram panchayats, in improving their capacity as gram panchayat members and in making gram panchayats pro-poor and people-centred, to represent the interests of the poor in decision-making bodies at various levels.

The emergence of NGOs as important development actors in India implies that one can hope for more attention to the needs and concerns of the poor in policy formulation and implementation. This raises a number of questions. What has been the experience of NGOs in generating and facilitating the possibilities for the poor to exert influence on political and economic processes? How are their intervention strategies designed? Are the intervention strategies based on factors that historically generated poverty? Are they based on the condition and severity of poverty across different villages and different poverty groups within a village? Have they succeeded in enabling a political discourse in which poverty and poverty reduction are significant issues? Have they facilitated social and political practices among the poor so that decision-making, agendas, policy and programme implementation, etc., can be influenced at the local level?

The Objectives

The objectives of the study are to:

1. analyse the magnitude and severity of poverty and the processes generating poverty in the selected villages;
2. examine the efforts made by the NGOs in alleviating poverty and to learn lessons in this regard;
3. examine the efforts made by line departments, panchayat raj institutions at the village level and other agencies such as banks and credit cooperatives; and
4. analyse the strategies adopted by the poor in coming out of poverty.

The central hypothesis guiding the study is that while the poor must be central actors in any attempt to bring about a reduction in the poverty condition, the endogenous development of the poor by the poor is not possible. The structural nature of poverty and the structures and processes of development require that the actions of the poor be supported by those of the state and other agencies in order to secure the rights, and policies that can benefit the poor and secure their development. The case study method has been used to analyse the objectives of the study.

The study was undertaken in villages covered by SHARE (Self-Help Association for Rural Education) and Sanghamitra Service Society (Sanghamitra, hereafter). The selection was based on the strategy of development and spatial location of the NGO. SHARE is a membership based organisation (but registered as NGO) working for the empowerment of its women members through an income generation activity in about 40 villages in a block in Vellore district (formerly part of North Arcot district) in Tamil Nadu State. Three villages were selected in consultation with the NGO; was two of them (Sabthalipuram and Mottupalyam), the NGO was working, and in another (Melvallam) it was not working. Sanghamitra is a registered society working in 14 villages in one mandal in Krishna district of Andhra Pradesh. Here also, three villages were selected in consultation with the NGO. In Bathinapadu and Kothapeta, the NGO was working, while in S. Amaravaram the NGO was not working.

The selection of NGOs was guided by the following. In India, NGOs have first emerged as important actors in southern part, and most of them are medium in size (covering 40-50 villages) in one or two taluks in a district. Both the NGOs fall into this category. Since the study involved a long-term association, the willingness of NGOs to become part of the study and learn in the process was important.

The cases of SHARE and Sanghamitra are appropriate for the purpose of analysing the role of NGOs in enabling the poor to gain economic and political space for poverty reduction for the reason that the NGOs are not interested in 'projectism' but are initiating a process towards the empowerment of the poor. Secondly, they seek to provide information and knowledge and other resources for their empowerment. The case of SHARE is particularly interesting because this is a membership based organisation which seeks to empower its women members by initiating activities aimed at income generation and empowerment. Secondly, as a membership based organisation, it involves members in planning, implementation and monitoring of all the development activities. This means that the organisation is to be accountable (as defined by Edwards and Hulme 1995) to its members, and it has to adopt principles of good governance, transparency and simple style of functioning. Thirdly, unlike most of the NGOs in India, SHARE first initiated an economic activity to enhance employment and income for its women members, and subsequently, formed Self-Help Groups (SHGs) in micro-finance among them, and other poor in the villages.

Notes

1. NGOs now have better space to collaborate with the government and influence the policy at different levels. The government has been discussing with prominent NGO leaders about the ways and means by which collaboration between the government and NGOs can be improved. Some prominent NGO leaders have found a place in key decision-making bodies, committees, etc. As a part of the preparatory process for the Ninth Five Year Plan, the government constituted several task forces in which one or two NGO leaders were included. Several ministries and departments in the Central Government and most of the state governments are actively seeking the views of NGOs in the formulation of policies and programmes. The central and federal governments have formulated various programmes in which NGOs can play an important role in either implementing them or enabling the poor to access them (Reddy and Rajasekhar 1996; Rajasekhar and Reddy 1997).
2. It is difficult to estimate the exact number of NGOs engaged in development work. One estimate is based on the registration with the Ministry of Home Affairs. For receiving any kind of assistance from international donors, NGOs should get themselves registered under the Foreign Contributions Regulation Act (FCRA), 1976, with the Ministry of Home Affairs. There are about 20,000 NGOs registered under FCRA. Since educational and charitable institutions are also required to have FCRA, one can assume that 50 per cent of them are assumed to be active in rural and urban development. There are also NGOs, without FCRA registration, which undertake developmental activities with assistance from the government and local contribution. If we include these organisations, the number is likely to be more than 20,000.

2

The Concepts of Poverty and Poverty Alleviation Strategies

Introduction

Development may be seen as a process by which the options are increasingly available to the poor to have access to resources towards improving their living conditions. Therefore, development interventions would become most effective and appropriate if they are based on an understanding of poverty (dimensions and causes), and strategies pursued by the poor and development actors to combat poverty. The most promising and/or successful strategies adopted by the poor and development actors can become foundations/role models on which development interventions are based.

The Concept of Poverty

Poverty is a concept that "describes the general condition of people who are badly off and encompasses many aspects of want and disadvantages" (Chambers 1988:3). However, what precisely are these wants and disadvantages is always debated. Very frequently, poverty is related to inadequate incomes (poverty line). Dreze and Sen (1989:15) describe poverty as a severe failure of basic capabilities. In their approach, a distinction is made between 'ends' (capabilities) and 'means' (low incomes or other causal antecedents of failures in basic capabilities). Chambers (1988 and 1995) criticises that the above do not directly consider the perceptions of the 'actors' themselves who may have a different understanding of deprivation and their own priorities. He suggests that five clusters of disadvantages (lack of assets, physical weakness, isolation, vulnerability and powerlessness) characterise the poor in rural areas. The poor themselves perceive that there are three priorities, namely, survival, security and self-respect; the last being their highest priority (Chambers 1988).

The conventional approach concentrates on income and/or consumption of the household to describe poverty as the inability of certain sections of the society to obtain income to meet the basic necessities. This conceptualisation of poverty suffers from the shortcomings (Murthy and Rao 1998) of:

(i) viewing market as a neutral institution to which all sections of the population have equal access and within which all sections can negotiate on an equal footing. In reality, markets reflect and perpetuate inequalities in society on the basis of class, caste, gender and other social relations;
(ii) prioritising the market as the main institutional mechanism for meeting the basic needs, and ignoring other institutional mechanisms for addressing these[1];
(iii) ignoring the institutional barriers which prevent certain sections of the poor, like women[2], *dalits* (untouchables)[3], tribals[4] and minority groups, from converting enhanced income into enhanced access to basic needs; and
(iv) ignoring intra-household inequalities which lead to unequal distribution of "household" income based on gender, age and physical ability.[5]

Chart 2.1, by taking the above into account, elaborates the concept of poverty by including common property resources (CPRs) and state provided commodities (SPC). Line 4 in Chart 2.1 adopts a somewhat broader definition which aims to capture the vulnerability of the poor by including assets (like human and physical capital, etc.,) which create a buffer between production, exchange and consumption which may be called upon during times of crisis (Swift 1989). The addition of dignity and autonomy in lines 5 and 6 incorporates still broader meaning of poverty including people's freedom from the necessity to perform activities that are regarded as subservient and their ability to choose self-fulfilling and rewarding lifestyles.

Chart 2.1: A pyramid of poverty concepts

1	....	PC
2.	....	PC + CPR
3.	....	PC + CPR + SPC
4.	....	PC + CPR + SPC + ASSETS
5.	.....	PC + CPR + SPC + ASSETS + DIGNITY
6.	....	PC + CPR + SPC + ASSETS + DIGNITY + AUTONOMY

Notes: PC: Per capita consumption
CPR: Common property resources
SPC: State provided commodities

Source: Baulch (1996).

Thus, to be poor implies principally:

- an inability to obtain the basic needs (food, shelter, health, etc.) as a consequence of low income and insufficient access to productive resources and assets, for instance, land;
- lack of opportunities to exploit human resources owing to insufficient access to education and health care;
- isolation[6] owing to physical conditions and/or inadequate education;
- lack of status and power[7], making it difficult to influence one's own situation and break out of poverty; and
- a high degree of vulnerability[8] owing to lack of productive assets, exposure to natural disasters, etc.

It needs to be, however, noted that poverty is not a static phenomenon, and it changes over time. The concept of poverty changes with time and across the regions. It also changes within individual economic groups and at various economic levels within a country, including at the household level where there would be considerable difference in the perceptions of women and men. The poor are not a homogeneous group with common interests and views.

Poverty has various dimensions. A distinction is to be made between absolute and relative poverty. Absolute poverty refers to lack of basic necessities. The relative poverty implies how poverty is perceived in relation to the condition of others in the society and how such a perception affects their own actions to come out of poverty.

Causes of Poverty

Poverty is the result of several failures. These failures have been classified by Sen (1981) as endowment failures, production failures and exchange failures (Chart 2.2). Subsequently, consumption failures have also been added as important contributing factors.

Chart 2.2 : Failures leading to poverty

Type of failure	How does it get reflected?
Endowment failures	Productive assets (private/common) Physical power Membership in the household and community citizenship in the state
Production failures	State of physical environment Skills and capacities Lack of inputs (credit, materials, etc.)
Exchange failures	Market prices for goods Employment options and wages Claims on household/community Claims on the state
Consumption failures	Drinking and other vices Intra-household decision-making Indebtedness

Chart 2.2 makes a point that poverty can result because of any of the failures. For instance, lack of land (endowment failure) can result in poverty. But, even if a household owns land, poverty can result due to production failures like low productivity or lack of access to inputs. Third dimension is that if there is no failure in endowment and production, poverty is still a possibility due to exchange failures (such as low prices for products, etc.).

All these failures result because of patriarchy, social inequality, structural problems, government policies, failures of institutions (both government and non-government) and policies of global institutions. It needs to be noted that it is the women, *dalits*, *adivasis* and landless households who are most disadvantaged under the influence of four types of failures. They are also discriminated by the society, government and institutions. The policies of global institutions can have an adverse impact on women. Thus, the main cause of poverty can be seen as shortfalls in the ownership, entitlements, endowments, production and exchange options for the poor and different poverty groups, due to their weak bargaining power within the existing social relations and institutions.

Poverty Alleviation Strategies

For analytical purposes, one can identify four dimensions of poverty: lack of assets, resources, knowledge and rights. Assets cover material possessions. Resources cover access to credit, education, health, drinking water, etc. Knowledge covers information that shapes the cognitive world ranging from technology to political ideas. And, finally, rights embrace social, political, economic, etc., legal and traditional (Pedersen and Webster 1998: 5).

The research[9] suggests that there are two main groups of strategies through which the poor can achieve a change in their conditions of poverty. First, there are strategies that are carried out by the poor in an attempt to change their poverty in terms of their resources and assets. Secondly, there are strategies through which the poor, or those representing the poor, seek to secure their interests by effecting change in the actions and policies of others and, in particular, bringing about change in public policy and in its implementation.

The former is often analysed in terms of the coping strategies of the poor. It is usually based upon individual or local groups of poor seeking ways to offset the economic disadvantages they face by exploiting opportunities to utilise the resources and assets they possess or can access. Migration, grass roots production co-operatives, loans from relatives or credit associations, diversification of production and entering new labour markets are some examples.

The second group of strategies is characterised by the need to change the policies and practices of others in order to bring about change. In particular, it is directed at achieving a redistribution of resources in order to change the poverty condition. Here, an important focus is upon effecting institutional change in terms of the formulation and implementation of policies. In terms of resources, this represents an attempt to change the basis upon which existing resources are distributed and utilised within the locality, and upon which new resources might be introduced into the locality and distributed. The discussion of poverty reduction thereby becomes one of mobilisation, organisation, representation, and empowerment.

A distinction between poverty alleviation and poverty reduction, therefore, becomes very pertinent. While the former concentrates on those assets and resources that have a bearing on the livelihood of the poor, the latter focuses on knowledge and rights. Thus, while agricultural growth and better access to markets can alleviate poverty, the involvement of the poor in development efforts becomes crucial for poverty reduction.

This way of looking at the impact of a programme on poverty necessitates an examination of four sets of indicators. These are livelihoods, resources, knowledge and rights. These have been summarised in Chart 2.3. It needs to be noted that these indicators need to be dis-aggregated by gender, caste and class.

Past Poverty Alleviation Strategies and Interventions

After independence, the perception of the Indian Government on development changed, and also the growth and role of NGOs in rural development (Rajasekhar 2000). During 1950s and 1960s, it was assumed that the state-led capital intensive economic growth in the industrial and agricultural sectors was the answer to poverty through trickle-down effect, accompanied by community development and welfare programmes for those groups (poor, poorest, women, etc.), which were thought to be incapable of participating in the programmes aimed at economic growth. The land reforms programme was also initiated which had a varying degree of success across the states (Box 2.1). The Government set up the Central Social Welfare Board and Khadi and Village Industries Commission to channel funds to the NGOs for implementing welfare programmes (health, education, shelter homes for the destitute, old age homes, etc.) and vocational programmes. Christian based aid agencies supported the work of Missionaries involved in welfare activities with a focus on health and education especially in South India and tribal areas of Central and Eastern India.

Chart 2.3 : Indicators of poverty reduction

Areas	What to look for?	Specific variables
Livelihoods	Ranging from improvement to impoverishment	• Employment of men, women and children. • Work-load on women • Income generating activities (regular or seasonal?) • Quality of work • Food security (seasonal?) • Ownership of assets
Resources	Ranging from access to exclusion	• Access to productive assets, markets, credit, land, irrigation • Access to communication facilities, water and sanitation • Access to training • Dependency on CPRs • Safety nets and social networks • Distribution of resources • Affordability of school fees • Affordability of health care • Free time for women
Knowledge	Ranging from expansion to reduction	• Children's school attendance • Community health care, health and education levels of women • Acquisition of technical, managerial, marketing, leadership skills • Coping mechanisms
Rights	Ranging from participation to alienation	• Greater participation in local organisations • Were the poor better organised or more assertive in their access or entitlement to rights • Property rights and women's land rights • Legal status • Reproductive rights • Respect from authorities • Personal security

During the 1960s, it was found that economic growth-oriented strategies, combined with welfare activities at the micro-level, were not adequate to alleviate poverty. In this context, the United Nations called for a frontal attack on poverty through the basic needs strategy.

By 1970s, the Indian Government initiated Small and Marginal Farmer Development Programmes with a view to alleviating poverty. Subsequently, many direct anti-poverty programmes such as IRDP, NREP, etc., were initiated (See Annex 2.1).

Box 2.1: Land reforms programme in India
In order to solve the problem of assetlessness, the government tried to implement a massive land reforms programme consisting of abolition of intermediaries, tenancy reforms and ceiling laws. The ceiling laws, first introduced in 1960s, were intended to acquire the land above ceiling fixed (which differed across various agro-climatic regions) and redistribute the same among landless households. Less than 3 million hectares of land was declared as surplus, which is too low a figure compared to surplus land estimated by various nation-wide surveys. Of this, only 1.8 million hectares of land was redistributed; further, landed households were significant beneficiaries of such redistribution. The tenancy reforms introduced in 1950s and 1960s, in fact, resulted in a large-scale eviction of small tenants and contributed to a rapid growth of agricultural labourers. Thus, tenancy reforms and ceiling laws were largely a failure. Though the government has admitted that the land reform process came to a "dead end", the scope to redistribute land among the landless by way of effective implementation of the existing ceiling laws still exists.

Simultaneously, during this period, alternative perspectives on development and role of NGOs were also emerging. In the early 1970s, a large number of young people and a section of intelligentsia with Marxist perspective of society, economy and development sought to organise the poor and the exploited in rural areas. What mattered at that time was class polarisation, and rich exploiting the poor. The issues such as gender, environment, human rights, sustainable development, etc., did not find much place in the political vocabulary. On the contrary, these terms were thought to be alien ideas imposed by the Capitalist world.

In mid-1970s, the Lohiaites and Gandhians came together under Jayaprakash Narayan and launched a total revolution movement for wiping out corruption, unemployment, exploitation. As a consequence, emergency was clamped all over the country by the then government. These developments paved the way for the emergence of NGOs working around issue based struggles (often referred to as social action groups) in different parts of the country (Stephen 1990). These social action groups focused upon issues such as price rise, emergency rule, corruption, deficiencies in the implementation of land reforms, and inability to enforce minimum wages.

By mid-1970s, the impact of Marxism was felt on the Church. With the advent of liberation theology, there was a split in the Church based institutions and Paul Freire's 'Pedagogy of the Oppressed' became the bible for dissenters within the Church. Further, the Janata Party's rise to power in 1977 raised hopes among the poor as well as in social action groups. This hope was soon dispelled as the new Government did not take a clear-cut stand on critical economic and political issues, and collapsed in 1979. As a result, the social action groups lost faith in the ability of the formal political processes to bring about transformation in the society. The early 1980s also witnessed the emergence of ideas on the need for people's participation, conscientisation and empowerment in poverty alleviation, as well as the need to take the diversity among the poor on the basis of class, caste, gender, ethnicity, etc., into account (PRIA 1991). Thus, the post-emergency period witnessed the people coming out of the Church, and the Left, Gandhian and Lohiaite movements getting converged as far as development at the grass roots level was concerned. They focused on awareness and conscientisation with the objective of mobilising the poor to influence the social, economic and political structure. Although many social action groups did not want to carry on the mobilisational work with external (foreign) support, a large number of other types of NGOs started availing external support.

By early eighties, the government gave considerable importance to banking sector in direct poverty alleviation, by fixing targets in achieving the desired direction in lending activities. The banks, which were by then nationalised, were asked to play a social role, and priority sector norms were introduced. The banks, however, could not effectively play the social role, and by 1980s, the viability of the banking sector itself became doubtful with growing proportion of overdues and costs outweighing returns (Annex 2.2).

Pragmatism combined with the need to improve the life situation of the poor soon made the people and activists from different backgrounds to talk of development by mid-1980s. The fragmented and compartmentalised development models which still had charity and welfare components were replaced by integrated development models. The gender justice, environmental concerns and human rights were understood as part and parcel of structural aspects of the society which, together with class, caste and ethnicity, were responsible for the exploitation of the marginalised sections within the society. The priorities and agenda of donor agencies also influenced the development perspective and programmes at the grass roots level (Rajasekhar 1998).

These trends contributed to the emergence of two distinct types of grass roots NGOs. Development NGOs sought to work around concrete sectoral activities relevant to different poverty groups in the countryside (agriculture, watershed, environment, off-farm and non-farm income generation activities, health, literacy, etc.). Although the charity and welfare NGOs were undertaking these activities, the crucial difference was that development NGOs sought to adopt participatory and innovative approaches. The other type of NGOs that came into existence was empowerment NGOs which formed organisations for different poverty groups in the countryside and strengthened their efforts to address the structural causes of their poverty. The main difference between social action groups and empowerment NGOs is that the latter are not transient, do not focus on a single issue, and are not averse to accepting foreign funding. Thus, by late 1980s there were four different grass roots NGOs which often co-existed in the same locality: welfare NGOs, development NGOs, empowerment NGOs and social action groups. While the first two types of the groups often entered into collaboration with the government, the last two often confronted state policies, legislations and practices. Support and network NGOs also emerged during the late 1980s, to lend capacity enhancement support to grass roots NGOs and create a platform for NGOs to meet, share experiences and carry out coordinated action (Murthy and Rao 1998).

The development NGOs were called upon by international aid agencies and Indian government to supplement the government's micro-level poverty alleviation and basic needs programmes in spheres where development NGOs were perceived to have comparative advantages. These comparative advantages are—reaching the poor, eliciting and enabling people's participation, promoting innovative and cost-effective approaches to poverty alleviation, identifying and disseminating appropriate technology, making the government's delivery system accountable, etc. Thus, a broader role was perceived by the Indian government for NGOs. For the first time, the Planning Commission included a separate sub-section on 'Involvement of Voluntary Agencies' in the Seventh Five Year Plan document (1985-1990) under the chapter on Rural Development and Poverty Alleviation Programmes. Plan expenditure of Rs. 100-150 crores was earmarked towards collaboration between the government and NGOs. To channel these resources for NGOs involved in poverty alleviation and rural development programmes, the Council for Advancement of People's Action and Rural Techno-logy (CAPART) was established in 1986. This agency was also entrusted with the responsibility of providing support to the NGOs.

By 1990s, significant developments started taking place in India and across the world. NGOs have now become popular with government and aid agencies in response to certain developments in economic and political thinking (Edwards and Hulme 1995 and 1996). The development policy of the World Bank, bilateral and multi-lateral agencies, and aid transfers from them, have come to be dominated by what is referred to as 'New Policy Agenda', which gives a prominent role to the NGOs in poverty alleviation and the development of civil society (Robinson 1993). The agenda has two elements—economic and political.

A serious balance of payments crisis occurred in 1991 due to increased government expenditure (owing to the growing size of government, mis-management of direct anti-poverty programmes, unproductive subsidies, etc.) and stagnant income (owing to a rigid licensing system, unhelpful tax structure and inability to raise internal resources through progressive taxation). The economic agenda, followed in India since 1991, sees the markets and private sector as efficient in producing the goods, services and in achieving rapid economic growth (Rajasekhar 1998). Liberalisation, globalisation and privatisation of the economy are the key elements of this agenda. The economic growth is considered as a key strategy for the poverty alleviation. However, the strategy proposed to achieve the economic growth is different to the one promoted in the 1970s. It is market-led rather than state-led, export-oriented rather than import-substitution-oriented, labour intensive rather than capital intensive, and women inclusive rather than women exclusive.

The aid agencies prescribed that Indian government should gradually reduce its role in service provision and development, and leave this task to the decentralised government and NGOs, as the latter are seen as cost-effective and efficient service providers. Indian government also called upon to implement local government programmes rather than supplementing them in their project areas. This new policy on NGOs is consistent with the overall emphasis of structural adjustment programmes which emphasise on cutting the role of government and privatisation of services.

In accordance with the above, the Indian Government provided favourable conditions for the decentralisation of government through the 73rd Constitutional Amendment[10] in 1993 (See Annex 2.3 for critical issues in decentralisation in India). Another important development in the 1990s was the assignment of an increasing role to NGOs by the government and external donors in service provision and poverty alleviation. The once insignificant NGOs today play a major role in coming up with different approaches and strategies aimed at poverty alleviation. The political space now available for the NGOs[11] is the result of the growth of NGO sector, which is, to a large extent, supported by external donors. The gradual recognition by the state of the possibilities and the potential of involving the NGO sector in anti-poverty programmes has enhanced the legitimacy of NGOs. Interface with the state and government agencies at different levels (Rajasekhar and Reddy 1997; Reddy and Rajasekhar 1996) has been found very useful in advocating policy changes in favour of the poor, although it is not a smooth process.

With the growth of NGOs and plenty of opportunities to involve in the non-governmental sector from early 1990s, lot of people with professional background and academic qualification and experience of working in the government joined the development stream. Such a development is also to be seen in the context of the increased need to professionally manage the poverty alleviation programmes for better results and impact. With increasing legitimacy and demand on the NGOs together with the flow of large money, issues of good governance, transparency, accountability, democracy, collectivity, etc., have become the agenda of development debate.

Magnitude, Trends and Dimensions of Poverty in India

Based on the poverty line approach[12], it is estimated that 23 per cent of the country's population lived below the poverty line in 1999-

2000 (Dev 2002: 46). While the proportion of the poor in rural areas was 24 per cent, in urban areas it was 22 per cent[13].

During the post-independence period, poverty trends seem to have proceeded in three distinct phases. First, the period from early 1950s to mid-1970s was characterised by fluctuations in poverty without any clear trend in either direction. Second, the incidence (severity and depth) of poverty steadily declined during the period 1971 to 1990. Third, from late 1980s, poverty appears to have entered into new phase of fluctuations[14] probably due to macro-economic reforms introduced in 1991[15]. There are contradicting studies on the impact of reforms on the poverty (Bhalla 2002 and Dev 2002). The incidence of poverty varies across the states, and within each state. According to income poverty statistics, the poor are concentrated in central and eastern states of India. If poverty is seen in non-material deprivation, it spreads to many other states. For instance, Tamil Nadu, Andhra Pradesh and Karnataka, which are better-off in terms of income poverty, are worse-off in terms of human development and gender development indices[16].

Poverty has ethnic, caste and gender dimensions. Tribals, while comprising 18 per cent of the total population, account for 27 per cent of the India's poor. Fifty per cent of the *adivasis* belong to the category of poor. They also suffer from non-material deprivation such as high illiteracy and drop-out rates. *Dalits* (persons belonging to depressed castes), while comprising 11 per cent of India's population, account for 15 per cent of India's poor. Most of the poor belonging to these communities are either landless or marginal farmers.

Women in India have improved their well-being in the last 30 years (Table 2.1) in terms of increased expectation of life at birth, increased age at marriage, gross enrolment ratio at all levels of education, work participation rate and organised employment, reduced infant mortality rate and less gap between infant mortality rate for girls and boys. Yet, poverty in India has gender dimension. With higher maternal and infant mortality rates, lower age at marriage, widespread illiteracy, higher drop-out rate from schools and lower work participation rates, Indian women are one of the most disadvantaged groups in the society. While in overall terms, women seem to have even better life expectancy and lesser death rates than men, more women die than men up to age 34. Infant and child

Table 2.1: Selected developmental indicators relating to women and children

	Before			After		
Indicators	Total	Female	Male	Total	Female	Male
Demography						
Population (in millions)	548.1	364.1 (1971)	284.0	1027 (2001)	495.7	531.3
Decennial Growth	24.6	24.9 (1971)	24.4	21.34 (1991-01)	21. 79	20.93
Vital Statistics						
Sex Ratio	—	930 (1971)	—	—	933 (2001)	—
Expectation of Life at Birth (years)	50.9 (1971)	50.2	50.5	62.9 (1996-01)	63.4	62.4
Mean Age at Marriage (years)	—	17.2 (1971)	22.4	—	19.4 (1995)	22.0
Health						
Birth Rate	36.9 (1971)	—	—	26.1 (1999)	—	—
Death Rate	15.7 (1970)	15.6	15.8	8.7 (1999)	8.3	9.0
Infant Mortality Rate	127 (1978)	131	123 (1999)	71.6 (1998)	72.0 (1997)	70.0 (1997)
Child Mortality Rate	127 (1978)	131	123	—	36.7 (1998-99)	24.9 (1998-99)
Maternal Mortality	—	468 (1990)	—	—	408 (1997) 540 (1998-99)	—
Literacy and Education						
Literacy Rates	16.7 (1971)	21.97	24.9	65.4 (2001)	54.2	75.9
Gross Enrolment Ratios						
Classes I-V	100.1	85.5	113.9	89.7	81.2	97.7
Classes VI-VIII	62.1	47.8 (1990-91)	76.6	58.5	49.5 (1997-98)	66.5

(contd.)

1	2	3	4	5	6	7
School Drop-out Rates						
Classes I-V	42.6	46.0	40.1	39.6	41.3	38.2
Classes VI-VIII	60.9	65.1 (1990-91)	59.1	54.1	58.6 (1997-98)	50.7
Work and Employment						
Work Participation	34.3	14.2 (1971)	52.8	37.7	22.3 (1991)	51.6
Women in the Organized Sector (in lakhs)	107.3 (1971)	8.6 (8.0%)	155.6	283.9 (1999)	44.4 (17.4%)	234.5 (1999)
Women in the Public Sector (in lakhs)	107.3	8.6 (8.0%) (1971)	98.7	194.3 (1996)	28.1 (14.5%) (1999)	167.9 (1996)
Women in Government (in lakhs)	109.0	11.9 (11.0%) (1981)	97.1	107.7 (1999)	16.3 (15.13%) (1999)	91.4
Decision-Making						
Women in the Administration (actual no. in IAS, IFS & IPS)	7102	413 (5.8%) (1987)	6689	8611	650 (7.6%) (1997)	7961
Women in the Panchayats (in lakhs)	8.67	2.92 (33.7%) (1995) #	5.75	27.21	7.25 (26.64%) (2001)	19.96
Women in the Parliament (actual no.)	768	47 (6.1%) (1989)	721	790	67 (8.4%) (1999)	723
Women in the Central Council of Ministers (actual no.)	40 -	4 (10%) (1985)	36	73	8 (10.9%) (1999)	65

Note: Figures in parenthesis indicate the percentage to the total, as also the year of the data in respective columns wherever relevant. Although efforts were made to keep a common 'base' and a common 'comparable' year, the same could not be kept up because of the limitations in the availability of data and other practical problems.

Data refers to only in respect of 7 States, viz., Haryana, Karnataka, Madhya Pradesh, Punjab, Rajasthan, Tripura and West Bengal between 1993 and 1995. Whole of India.

Source: Gopalan 2002.

mortality rates are higher for girls than boys. Deprivation in literacy is significantly more among women. More girls drop out even at the primary stage of education than boys (Gopalan 2002: 330).

Further, the quality of employment leaves much to be desired. Over 90 per cent of the rural women workers are unskilled and hence, they are mainly engaged in informal/unorganised sector. Wage rates for women in agriculture are, on an average, 30-50 per cent less than those for men. Women shoulder almost the entire burden of household activities and childcare responsibilities, and a large proportion of women's work time is spent in such activities. Female casual labourers in rural India show the highest incidence of poverty of any occupational category, male or female. Women-headed households suffer from a disproportionate burden of poverty. At the same time, the delivery structures of credit, technical advice, etc., do not reach them because of their gender bias. The employment of women in the organised and public sectors is much lower than that for men. The presence of women in decision-making positions is nowhere near parity with men. The National Commission for Women observes that with the shrinking development expenditure owing to growing debt and interest burden on both central and state governments, the axe generally fell on social sectors including women development (Gopalan 2002: 22).

To address both material and non-material dimensions of poverty, as discussed in the previous section, the Indian Government embarked upon economic growth-oriented strategies combined with micro-level welfare activities since 1950s. The Green Revolution introduced in late 1960s ensured self-sufficiency in food production; but did not bring equitable distribution of benefits to the poor. In order to have a direct impact on poverty, several direct anti-poverty programmes [such as Integrated Rural Development Programme (IRDP)] were initiated all over India. All these programmes gave preference to tribals, depressed castes and women. Furthermore, commercial banks were nationalised in 1969, and were directed to play a social role by shedding their commercial sector. The concept of priority sector lending was introduced in the mid-1970s to ensure adequate flow of credit to the needy and poor at subsidised rates of interest. These programmes contributed to poverty alleviation to some extent; but sustainable poverty alleviation did not take place[17] due to lack of congruence between delivery and recipient systems, absence of people's organisations, and lack of co-ordination between various government departments implementing the anti-poverty programmes leading to overlapping, duplication, and so on. As far as the credit from commercial banks for poverty alleviation is concerned, the proportion of the poor obtaining credit from the formal banks has been lower than their share in the total population (Annex 2.2).

The government also brought in reforms in decentralised governance in India (Annex 2.3). Further, donors and the government seek to involve NGOs in poverty alleviation. In this context, it would be interesting to analyse the poverty alleviation strategies. In the next chapter, we look into the methodology adopted in the study.

Notes

1. In reality, people meet their basic needs through a variety of other resources. Poor people claim free food, clothing and shelter from kith and kin in times of crisis, use free fruits and fodder from Common Property Resources (CPRs). They also avail of the nutrition programmes and health and education services of government organisation, however inadequate they are. In fact, the livelihood strategies of the poor, particularly women, involve not just an engagement with income generating activities or the labour market, but also social networking, changes in consumption pattern, labour and asset pooling, savings, borrowing, etc.
2. Intra-household inequalities in the distribution of food, community norms and gender bias of the community (and also the government) reduce the poor women's ability to access the basic needs, even with increase in their income.
3. Caste based violence in different parts of India reveal the difficulty experienced by poor *dalits* in using their increased income through new sources of employment to expand access to education. Increased income has also not led to better access to drinking water for *dalits* where caste hierarchies restrict their access to common wells.
4. In the case of tribals, the barriers may not be community norms and practices, but practices of the state which has neglected infrastructural development in tribal areas.
5. Naila Kabeer (1996) argues that the conventional measures of income and well-being can only capture male poverty as they are premised on the notion of male actor and of the experience of male poverty. Further, per capita income emphasises on the households and hence, the intra- household inequality is overlooked. She identifies three disjunctures introduced by gender: translation of labour into income, income into choice and choice into personal well-being. Whether women are able to convert labour into income, income into choice, and choice into personal well-being depend

upon social norms and cultural contexts. Thus, only when research focuses on context-specific analysis can one be able to find out whether gender inequality is offset, exacerbated, or unaffected by scarcity.

6. Isolation refers to being peripheral and cut off. Poor people can be isolated geographically—living in a 'remote' area; isolated in communication, lacking contacts and information, including not being able to read; isolated in lack of access to social services and markets; and isolated in lack of social and economic supports.
7. *Powerlessness:* The poor are powerless. Dispersed and anxious as they are about access to resources, work and income, it is difficult for them to organise or bargain. Often physically weak and economically vulnerable, they lack influence. Subject to the power of others, they are easy to ignore or exploit.
8. The terms 'vulnerable' and 'poor' are often used as alternating synonyms. But vulnerability is not the same as income-poverty or poverty more broadly defined. It means not lack or want, but exposure and defencelessness. It has two sides: the external side of exposure to shocks, stress and risk; and the internal side of defencelessness, meaning a lack of means to cope without damaging loss, which can take many forms—becoming or being physically weaker, economically impoverished, socially dependent, humiliated or psychologically harmed. For hundreds of millions, vulnerability has increased, and so their livelihoods have become less securely sustainable, even when their incomes have risen. In most cultures and contexts, patron-client safety nets have weakened, the extended family gives less support, contingencies such as weddings, funerals, brideprice and dowry have become more costly, and effective health services have become less accessible or more expensive or both. More people have moved into insecure environments. More people live exposed to risk of famine, flood, storm, and some human, crop and animal diseases, than before. War and civil disorder remain widespread, and where there have been past disasters, many are more vulnerable through the earlier loss of livelihood assets and means to cope. It then takes less to meet a famine, as in the 1994 famine in Ethiopia. For poor people there are often trade-offs between income and security. Income-poverty thinking can neglect vulnerability in seeking to raise incomes. On a huge scale, the Integrated Rural Development Programme in India provides subsidised loans to poor people to acquire assets aimed at raising their incomes. But as many have experienced, this increases vulnerability: loss of the asset can lead to debt and being worse off than before. At the margin, poor people often prefer a lower income with less risk of debt and dependence.
9. Here, we refer to the research carried out by the Centre for Development Research, Copenhagen, on Local Organisations and Rural Poverty Alleviation.
10. The amendment provided positive discrimination for women, *adivasis* and *dalits*, made the five-year elections mandatory; sought to provide adequate flow of funds to several tiers of the decentralised government and set up accountability mechanism at various levels.
11. For theoretical formulation and empirical work in this regard, see, Webster

and Pedersen (2002).

12. In India, the official figures on poverty are based on nutritional baseline measured in calories (food-energy method). The Planning Commission defines the poverty line as per capita monthly expenditure of Rs. 49 for rural areas and Rs. 57 for urban areas at 1973-74 all-India prices. The poverty line corresponds to a total household per capita expenditure sufficient to provide a daily intake of 2,400 calories in rural areas and 2,100 calories in urban areas, and also basic non-food items such as clothing and transport. Individuals who fail to obtain income to meet even these basic necessities fall below the poverty line.
13. These figures have been obtained from Datt (1997).
14. These are, however, around a level considerably lower than that which prevailed in the 1970s.
15. The impact of liberalisation policies introduced in 1991 on poverty is a debated issue. It has been argued that the incidence of poverty increased in 1992 due to the introduction of macro-economic reforms. This has been, however, disputed by others (World Bank 1996:5). While it is difficult to come to any firm conclusion regarding the impact of macro-economic policies on poverty at the macro-level, the micro-level reality suggests that the livelihood options for the poor have come under severe stress and strain after 1991. See, Joshi *et al.* (1997), and various articles in the *Economic and Political Weekly* for more details.
16. The proportions of *dalits* (depressed castes) and *adivasis* (tribals) are relatively higher in Tamil Nadu and Andhra Pradesh. The incidence of child labour is the highest in Andhra Pradesh.
17. See, for instance, Rath (1985) and Rajasekhar and Vyasulu (1990).
18. The number of groups increased from 28,031 (with 4.69 lakh members) by the end of 1989-90, to 86,774 (with 14.96 lakh members) by November 1994. During this period, the achievement exceeded the target by more than 100 per cent (Rajakutty 1997: 91).
19. Organisations are defined as identifiable groups of individuals operating within a mutually recognized structure under an explicit mandate and having (i) prescribed modes of operation, and (ii) formally agreed individual roles. Institutions are defined as clusters of rules. These are both embedded in and surround organisations.
20. The centre is still maintaining power to set broad policy guidelines, exerting control over public expenditures, and responsible for coordination between decentralized bodies in the supply of key goods and services, in monitoring, and enforcement of property rights and rules.
21. The literature suggests that responsiveness to the poor is quite rare, even in successful cases of decentralisation, and it is determined mainly by the politics of local-central relations (between central and local elites). Positive outcomes are mainly associated with strong commitment by a national government or a party to promoting the interests of the poor at the local level.
22. Capture is when those who manage public services seek rents, not serving the public interest.

ANNEX 2.1

DIRECT POVERTY ALLEVIATION PROGRAMMES

Employment Programmes

To promote employment opportunities to the poor, the government introduced the Crash Scheme for Rural Employment (CSRE) and Drought-Prone Area Programme (DPAP) in 1970s. The total number of work-days generated by CSRE was 178 million, while DPAP generated 37.9 million work-days of employment. However, the proportion of amount spent on these programmes to total plan outlay was generally low. Further, wages as a proportion to total expenditure was also low—especially under DPAP. Though these programmes were meant to provide employment to the 'most needy', targetting has been neither very specific nor very effective. Further, these programmes emphasised on building up of economic infrastructure such as roads, afforestation and markets, which only indirectly contributed to the welfare of the poor. Moreover, richer segments in rural areas subverted public works programmes to serve their own interests. Overall, these programmes could not provide long-term answers to the unemployment problem among the poor.

National Rural Employment Programme (NREP)

A nation-wide National Rural Employment Programme (NREP), instituted in 1980, aimed to utilise unemployed and underemployed labour in rural areas to create productive community assets. This programme focused not only on productive assets such as irrigation infrastructure, drainage systems, and soil conservation schemes, but also on basic social services such as wells, village schools, health sub-centres, and rural housing and roads. The total amount of expenditure for NREP increased from Rs. 15 billion during 1980-85 to, nearly, Rs. 22 billion during the period 1985-86. However, the employment generated by the NREP was only less than 8 per cent of total unemployment in 1980. Further, NREP was not meant to provide full-time year round employment; it merely attempted to supplement the income of the poor—especially during the slack season. Although it is difficult to assess the overall impact of NREP, it represents a major commitment on the part of the government to address the unemployment problem among the poor.

Jawahar Rozgar Yojana (JRY)

Jawahar Rozgar Yojana (JRY), which merged all the earlier employment programmes, is a major anti-poverty employment programme, which is managed and implemented by thousands of elected representatives. The primary objective of the JRY is generation of additional gainful employment for the unemployed and underemployed from among poorer groups. The other objectives are creation of community assets for the benefit of the poor and improvement in the overall quality of life. Notwithstanding the problems of inadequate resources, lack of people's involvement, poor implementation etc., this remains a major anti-poverty employment programme in the country today. The poor would benefit more if their organisations take an active part in the selection and implementation of the projects.

Integrated Rural Development Programme (IRDP)

The IRDP was initiated on a nation-wide basis in early 1980s to increase the income generating assets of the poor directly through a mixture of subsidies and credit. IRDP, which was allocated Rs. 15 billion during the period 1980-85 and Rs. 13.49 billion during the period 1985-89, was partially successful in lifting the rural poor above the poverty line. Many irregularities in the programme were reported and the space does not permit us to list all of them and the contributing factors. But, due to non-involvement of the people in the programme, the beneficiaries selected for the programme were not always the poorest. In cases where the community was involved in the selection process, the targetting and the impact of the programme tended to be better. This suggests that if the poor represent themselves in these programmes through their own organisations, the benefits of such a massive programme like IRDP can be enormous.

Minimum Needs Programme

Over the years, the government has sponsored a wide variety of programmes to make available certain minimum social services to all. A core group of these programmes—elementary education, adult education, rural health, rural water supply, rural electrification, rural roads, housing for the rural poor, and nutrition—are now being implemented through the MNP, which started in 1980. The programme is successful in providing facilities in rural areas; but the poor, in the absence of their own organisations, are unable to derive much benefit from these facilities.

Minimum Wages and Organisations of Labour

Wages paid to the agricultural labourers in India are low and do not leave any surplus over the cereal consumption for meeting other food and non-food needs. In this context, fixation, periodic revision and effective implementation of minimum wages become relevant. Though minimum wages are fixed in many states, their implementation is becoming difficult in the absence of strong organisations of agricultural labourers to assert their rights and an effective mechanism for implementation.

Provision of Agricultural Inputs and Subsidies

In order to stabilise domestic food production, and increase the productivity of small and marginal farmers, agricultural inputs such as credit, fertilisers, seeds, implements etc., are provided either at free of cost or at subsidized rates to small and marginal farmers.

Development of Women and Children in Rural Areas (DWCRA)

DWCRA is a sub-scheme of IRDP exclusively for women as women members of IRDP families did not receive adequate benefits. Under this programme, the government staff in a village would form a 15-member women's group, which, after regular monthly savings of Rs. 30 for six months, would be eligible for an interest free loan from a local formal bank (grant in the cases of *dalit* and *adivasi* women). Each successful repayment would make the group eligible to borrow higher amounts. The commercial banks were particularly attracted to this programme because lending was based on the savings of women members, and larger loans were be given only after the group proved itself through repayment. As a result the programme expanded rapidly[18]. Although the group formation process became short and *ad hoc*, and many programmes became inactive and defunct due to a 'lack of orientation of the project staff, inadequate staffing, poor follow-up, target chasing, (and) insufficient linkages' (Rajakutty 1997), a large number of NGOs enabled their groups to access resources from the DWCRA programme where loan assistance to women's groups was found to be relatively more productive than other social banking programmes, and repayments were better.

Merging of all the Anti-Poverty Programmes

All the anti-poverty programmes were merged into two programmes (SGSY and SGRY) in 1999. We do not have much evidence on the functioning of these programmes; but, the indications are that these are also going in the same direction as previous programmes on direct poverty alleviation.

ANNEX 2.2

FORMAL RURAL BANKING SYSTEM AND CREDIT COOPERATIVES IN INDIA

Formal Banks

The growth of Indian rural banking system consisting of Commercial Banks and Regional Rural Banks (RRBs) has been phenomenal after the nationalization of banks in 1969, and the subsequent bank branch expansion in rural areas. The total number of public sector bank branches increased from 6,596 in 1969 to 61,235 in 1993. The rural branches increased much more rapidly; while the total number of branches increased over six times, the rural branches increased by eighteen times. The growth of deposits and advances also kept pace, recording a steep increase. This ensures that the rural people are covered quite impressively for their investment credit and working capital requirements by the banking system. To improve access to credit for the rural poor, the state played a key role not only in the transformation of commercial banking into social banking but also in targetting credit through a number of subsidized credit programmes.

All this, however, did not produce the desired results. The spread of the banking system has been uneven across the regions (Nair 1991:31-4) and wealth groups (Tandon 1988:50-63; Rao 1980:90). The proportion of the poor obtaining credit from the banking system has been lower than their share in the total population because of the insistence on collateral which cannot be provided by them and a widespread belief that they are not bankable. Problems within the banking system such as complicated procedures, unimaginative lending policies and procedures, absence of provision for consumption credit, political interference, distant location, cultural gap between officials and borrowers, and short banking hours have also restricted the poor in gaining access to credit.

Even if some of the poor had obtained credit from the banking system, they found that the credit was neither timely nor adequate (Rajasekhar and Vyasulu 1990). Further, the interest and vocational training of a borrower had not been given due consideration while lending decisions were taken or while disbursing loans. Without sufficient knowledge of the activities for which loans were taken, the borrowers tended to misutilise the loan. There were also internal problems including absence of linkages of credit with marketing, investment credit having no provision for working capital etc. Added to these, lending small sized loans to a large number of borrowers increased transaction costs to all the banks. Finally, the managerial inadequacies within the banking system came in the way of providing timely and adequate credit.

These problems resulted in an alarming growth of overdues, which, in turn, adversely affected the recycling of credit, and led to lower profit margins. Many commercial banks and RRBs are either incurring losses or have become sick.

There has been mounting pressure from Indian bankers and some outside agencies that reforms are necessary to make the banking sector viable. Yielding to this pressure, the government appointed the Narasimham Committee in 1991, which recommended measures to improve the viability of the finance sector. Among these, one important recommendation is that the size of the priority sector lending should be gradually reduced in over three years, and then done away with it altogether. Though the government has yet to accept this recommendation, the proportion of credit disbursed under the priority sector has fallen well short of the stipulated target of 40 per cent of bank advances consecutively for the second time in 1992-93.

Credit Cooperatives in India

The credit cooperatives form an important component of rural credit delivery system in India. In the nine decades of their existence, they played a significant role in providing credit for agriculture and rural development. Initially, cooperatives were concerned with providing credit for short-term production. Later on, separate institutions were set up to provide investment loans to the farmers.

The structure of cooperative credit institutions providing short-term credit is as follows. At the lowest level, the Primary Agricultural Cooperative Societies (PACS) provide mainly credit though they are supposed to be multi-purpose in character. Farmers' Service (cooperative) Societies (FSS) are multi-purpose societies with larger area of operation and larger membership. In the tribal areas, Large-size Adivasi Multi-Purpose Societies (LAMPS) are expected to provide all types of credit and non-credit services (including marketing of agricultural and minor forest produce) under one single roof. Under three-tier structure, these primary societies are affiliated to District Central Cooperative Banks (DCCBs) at the district level which, in turn, are affiliated to the State Cooperative Banks (SCBs), referred to as apex banks, at the state level. In those states where two-tier structure exists, the primary societies are affiliated to the apex banks.

The structure of the cooperative credit institutions providing long-term investment credit differs, across the states. In most of the states, there is a federal structure under which the State Cooperative Agriculture and Rural Development Bank (SCARDB) at the state level is affiliated to Primary Agriculture and Rural Development Bank (PARDBs) at the district or taluk levels. In some states, there is unitary structure wherein the operational units below the SCARDB are its branches. In Andhra Pradesh, the short-term and long-term cooperative credit institutions have been integrated.

The share of credit cooperatives in the total institutional credit to the agricultural sector was more than 60 per cent in 1994-95, the largest within the existing multi-agency institutional structure. They are also important as far as geographical coverage, number of retail outlets, and membership coverage are concerned.

Notwithstanding their long existence and vast coverage, the cooperative credit institutions suffer from chronic problem of deterioration of their financial health. This can be attributed both to internal as well as external factors. Internal factors include poor resource base, high transaction costs, lack of business diversification, mounting overdues, lack of professionalism in management, faulty accounting procedures among the different tiers of cooperative institutions etc. External factors include state government controls with high degree of bureaucratization, multiplicity of control over these institutions, administered interest rate regime resulting in poor financial spreads, supersession of the boards of credit cooperatives etc. Further, the co-operative law has given overwhelming powers to the government to interfere in the operation of co-operatives, nullifying the benefits of mutual self-help and solidarity.

ANNEX 2.3

CRITICAL ISSUES IN DECENTRALISATION

Decentralisation implies transformation of many of the organisations and institutions involved in rural development.[19] Shifting project management and resource mobilisation from state bureaucracies to local elected governments and local organisations requires structural and procedural changes in both civil service and civil society. A key feature of these reforms is that they define new relationships between the state, local organisations and the individual, including the private sector and the market. A main rationale for the reforms arises from disillusionment with the performance of the state and implications of the costs that this has (and to some extent with the market) in addressing goals of rural development and poverty reduction. The focus on community organisations is considered to be important to foster more effective and accountable provision of services, management of resources and client responsive decision-making. Among other things, this shift in focus is expected to mobilise new or additional resources at local level that might have been under-utilised (labour, knowledge, capital and organisation). The building of local organisations and capacity is seen as a way out of the state-market dilemma.

In India, the 73rd and 74th Constitutional Amendments and subsequent State Acts created a policy environment conducive to decentralised governance and management of development activities. A significant proportion of donor supported rural development projects now include measures seeking to further government's efforts in administrative, fiscal and political decentralisation. Most state governments have been promoting varying combinations of three broad approaches in rural development:

- De-concentration of decision-making and improving internal management of line agencies to reorient the staff towards greater participation, transparency and accountability in service delivery, particularly in relation to the ultimate clients—rural men and women;
- Ceding responsibility for certain services and management functions and relying increasingly on alliances with NGOs, local user groups and private commercial organisations;

- Decentralisation and devolution of authority to local government as a measure to bring governance closer to people and improve rural resource mobilisation, service delivery and development.

Although evidence suggests a generally positive effect on development outcomes of these measures, the benefits of decentralisation and reforms in administrative structures remain very uneven. Recent evaluations suggest that in situations where communities are expected to play a major role in project implementation, examples of effective organisations are rare. In India, while policy change supports a potentially high degree of political decentralisation, devolution of administrative and fiscal responsibilities to local government remain an incomplete agenda in most states and sectors (World Bank 2000). Achievements in devolution of authority within line agencies to field-offices are mixed, as are efforts in creating better relationships between civil servants, clients and organisations at the local level (Saxena 2000). Challenged by deeply entrenched, authoritarian and frequently inequitable social practices the realities of India's efforts to bring about democratic governance as yet fall short of expectations.

A focus on decentralisation and community-driven development may bring both better governance and less market 'imperfections'. But this requires change at two levels. First, reform of state agencies (structure/decision-making, commitment, skills, attitudes) towards decentralised local governance, improved responsiveness and participation, which implies a shift in the locus of power from the centre to the periphery[20]. Second, rural people, including the poor, need to seize the new opportunities provided, and challenge the state and oppressive elites that maintain inequalities[21]. This raises a key issue regarding decentralisation; how to balance the locus of power between the centre and the periphery and develop accountability and responsiveness at central and local levels (encourage participation and voice; and limit exit, cooptation, and capture).[22]

Getting the balance between the centre and the periphery right—both in terms of the locus of power and in terms of regional/spatial and social distribution of benefits—requires an appropriate balance between a set of factors and relationships, e.g.:

- Degree of commitment to devolve powers to local actors and provision of administrative and financial resources to accompany the political process;
- Degree to which strategic central government control allows sufficient autonomy for local government; and more generally, provision of political, legal and administrative space for the emergence of community-driven civil society, and market-based organisations;
- Commitment to financial support, capacity building and policy advice for local government and support for civil society organisations; and
- Responsiveness to the poor and powerless groups.

3

Action Research Methods for Poverty Alleviation

Introduction

One of the objectives of the study was to build the capacity of the selected NGOs in finding the situation and needs of the poor, and enable them to prepare action plans in collaboration with the poor to alleviate poverty. Hence, the methodology of the study included building the capacity of the NGO teams in participatory data collection methods, and analysis of data leading to action. The role of ISEC was to ensure the quality of data and canvass the questionnaires. Thus, the methodology adopted was action research which became important in the following context.

Any intervention on poverty alleviation requires a thorough understanding of the processes that generate poverty. Such an intervention will have a good chance of success when it is designed on the basis of situation and needs of the poor. A poverty alleviation project must be able to answer the following questions before it is designed: Who are the poor? Why are they poor? What means do they adopt to overcome poverty? Which are the organisations involved in poverty alleviation in the locality? What are their poverty alleviation strategies? What is the impact of these strategies on poverty? What lessons can be learnt from these interventions? How to design an action plan by taking situation and needs of the poor into consideration? How will one involve government officials and representatives of local decentralised government in the discussions on development of action plans?

It is, thus, necessary to analyse the situation of the poor and assess their needs before a project is designed. This raises some questions: who should undertake the exercise? And, how? With regard to the question on *who* should undertake the exercise, the answer can be either the initiator of the project (such as government, NGOs, etc.) or the people for whom the project is being initiated. If the people, along with the initiators of the project, are involved in the project from the initial phase itself, the former will have more clarity on the linkages between their situation and needs, on the one hand, and the project design and its implementation, on the other. This contributes to their participation, more stakes and the ultimate success of the project.

How can one undertake the exercises on the situation analysis and needs assessment? What methodology should be adopted to enable the people to participate in the exercises? Given the widespread illiteracy and lack of formal education, this question becomes all the more important. The Participatory Rural Appraisal (PRA) appears to be the most suitable method to enable the rural poor to participate in situation analysis and needs assessment. But, following are the trade-offs:

- between quality considerations and time required for the exercises;
- between the number of exercises needed to collect authentic data and the time that the people and NGOs can spare; and
- between sequences of the exercises and keeping the interest of the people in them alive.

The design has to face these trade-offs, if people are to be involved right from the beginning. Given that people's participation is recommended by all the development actors (donors, government and NGOs) for the maximum success of a project, the following questions become pertinent: What exercises are to be conducted to analyse the situation and needs of the poor? What should be their sequence? What is the time that is normally required to complete all the exercises? What should be the process? How will these exercises help design a project?

To find out the answers to these questions, an Action Research Project (ARP) was undertaken as part of the study in the late 1997 with the support of GTZ/SHPAP in the project areas of two selected

NGOs. The objective was to enhance the institutional capacity of NGOs and Self-Help Groups (SHGs) to analyse different issues relating to poverty, contribute to the widened scope for sustained involvement of different types of poverty groups and ensure that their perspectives inform the policies and the concerned actions. Learning was in-built in this project to facilitate a continuous learning process where research lead to action; action lead to reflection; and, reflection lead to further research. This chapter documents the process adopted in the ARP, methodological issues and lessons.

The Preparation

The First Step

The first step was to share the idea with all the stakeholders to have a shared understanding of the objectives and the process that was going to be adopted, and thereby to achieve collective ownership on the very process itself.

The Process Adopted

Before initiating the ARP, a letter was sent by the GTZ/SHF to five partner NGOs located in Andhra Pradesh and Tamil Nadu states requesting their participation. Four agreed to take part and were invited to a one-day workshop in Bangalore to discuss the objectives, activities and methodology of the project. They were requested to take the idea of ARP back to their organisation, and share it with other stakeholders—the Governing Board, staff and target group. They were also requested to collectively decide the villages where the exercises should be conducted, and who among the stakeholders in an organisation should be part of the ARP. Criteria to select the villages and the team were collectively evolved. In view of the frequent turnover of the staff within an organisation, it was decided to include target group members (those SHG leaders who could read and write a little bit) in the team.

The ARP was undertaken only in the project areas of two NGOs as the partnership in the case of the other two was coming to a close for different reasons. Each of the NGOs sent a list of villages where ARP was to be undertaken. These villages were different in socio-economic terms. In the project area of SHARE, one village had urban influence, the second had irrigation, and was dominated by *dalits* and the third was highly politicised, and sharply divided along caste lines. Of the three villages chosen in the project area of Sanghamitra, one village was dominated by *dalits*, while the other two had multiple castes, and commercial agriculture. As far as the ARP team was concerned, SHARE sent a list of six members. Of them, two belonged to the target group, while the rest were staff. The team from Sanghamitra consisted of 11 persons, four of these persons were target group members, who had only primary education.

Problems Faced

- Leaving the decision to NGO leaders to select the team members from within their staff did not work out very well. The nature of work involved in ARP and requirements in terms of time, commitment, group work and motivation were not properly explained. The decision on the composition of the team was influenced by the availability and training needs of the staff. Further, the assumptions on the continuity of the staff went wrong. As a result, there was a high turnover leading to problems such as lack of continuity in terms of trained personnel and spending too much time to train the newcomers.
- Cohesiveness within the team was found to be lacking because of inter-personal relationships, resulting in group work suffering.
- A few staff members joined with the expectation of gaining mileage in terms of promotions and tenure. When they learnt that the ARP had nothing to do with the above, their motivation and commitment were affected.
- ARP was linked with the future GTZ/SHF support.

Learning Points

- Clarify that the ARP was related to situation analysis and needs assessment, and that it was not linked to funding.
- Start the ARP with a meeting where the nature of ARP, type of commitment needed and ownership of the project is explained to the entire organisation.

* Invite the voluntary participation of the staff. After considering commitment, motivation and capacity, prepare

a list of probable staff members in the team. The final selection should be left to the NGO.

Training Programme on Concepts and Methods

The objectives of this step were to: (i) explain the objectives, activities and expected outcome of ARP to the team members; (ii) familiarise them with concepts and causes of poverty, poverty alleviation strategies, local organisations and their characteristics; (iii) equip them in data collection through PRA techniques; (iv) prepare them to the fieldwork; (v) enable them to prepare a list of 'dos' and 'don'ts' during the fieldwork; and (vi) work out a method by which there was a possibility to have daily feedback and discussion during the fieldwork on the process adopted, problems encountered and how to sort out the problems.

The Process Adopted

The training programme began with a discussion on the objectives, activities and expected outcome of the ARP. At this stage, the team members had many questions on methodology, time that they might have to spend on the project, the expected impact and the utility of the project. These questions arose because the NGO leaders either did not explain the project or left out some crucial details.

This was followed by a discussion on poverty concepts. Although it was decided very early that the definition of poverty or a list on causes of poverty should not be imposed on the team members, this became inevitable. This was followed by a discussion on various data collection methods. In the training programme conducted in Krishna district, the problems that the team might face in the field were brought out through role-plays, practical examples, group work and rehearsals. All these classroom exercises resulted in preparing a list of 'dos' and 'don'ts' in PRA exercises (Box 3.1).

In Tamil Nadu, the team was taken for fieldwork on the last day of the four-day training programme to conduct wealth-ranking exercise. After a three-month break, training was provided on seasonality mapping and resource mapping before these were conducted in the field. As the staff were busy with organisational work, there was further delay in conducting the remaining exercises.

Box 3.1: Dos and Don'ts in conducting PRA exercises

Dos	Don'ts
• Advance preparation for the PRA meeting. • Ensuring clarity in questions. • Have patience (in the exercise) and listen (to people). • Have very good understanding of the topic on which PRA is conducted. For example, the facilitator conducting PRA on causes of poverty should have clarity on the distinction between causes and symptoms of poverty. • Discuss and decide the date and time (of PRA exercise) as per the convenience of the people in advance. • Develop skills to mobilise people for the meeting and ensure that the discussion is interesting. • Enable the people to develop self-confidence that they know, can participate and contribute to the exercises. • Should be attentive, sensitive, and sympathetic to people's opinions. • Follow good methods such as sitting on the ground along with the people and eating food along with them. • Know well in advance your role in the exercise. • Enable people to understand the complications that may arise in the usage of locally available things such as foodgrains and pulses, colour, beads, and *rangoli* powder. Select items that are locally available.	• Do not pose a second question without completely listening to the answer for the first question. • Do not condemn their answer. • Questions should not hurt and belittle them. • Should not laugh when they are explaining their problems. • Do not impose your ideology and views. • Do not complete the exercise in a hurried manner just because time is insufficient. Request whether you could go back some other time. • Do not give lengthy speeches. • Do not conduct PRA meetings in public places when sensitive information is to be collected. • Do not take notes in front of them.

In Andhra Pradesh, the team completed the exercises on social mapping and tested out the remaining soon after the training programme. But, there was, however, a gap between resource mapping and wealth ranking, and between wealth ranking and focus group interviews. This gap was considered essential as some of the team members were near illiterate, and needed some time to digest the information. Another reason for the gap was that the exercises were organically linked; for instance, until the results of wealth ranking were processed and analysed, the focus group interview on seasonality mapping, causes of poverty and poverty alleviation strategies could not be undertaken. Some unforeseen factors (floods and untimely rains) resulted in longer breaks in the process.

The Outcome

- Strengthened the analytical and reasoning capacity of the NGO team.
- The NGO team learnt the concepts, causes and dimensions of poverty, types of poverty alleviation strategies, the difference between political and individual strategies, and why the poor found it difficult to adopt certain strategies.
- In addition to inputs on local organisations and their characteristics, methods by which an organisation could be evaluated in terms of accountability, transparency, poverty commitment and efficiency were provided.
- A set of techniques (PRA, survey, interview and case study) was made available to establish rapport with the people, analyse their situation and needs.

Problems with the Process

- As the training on concepts and several methods took place in Tamil Nadu at different time points, the team could not see the continuity in the concepts and methods.
- The frequent turnover of staff implied that the composition of the team was different in each training programme, certain amount of repetition was essential and considerable time was spent for the training itself.
- There were different perceptions between the ISEC and NGO teams on the importance (in terms of time) to be given to learning and internalising the concepts, and to field-testing the concepts.
- For a number of reasons, there were delays between one

component of the ARP and another. This resulted in loss of continuity, the team members losing interest in the process and the villagers losing track of the process.

- Although not intended, the classroom inputs dominated the training programme.

Learning Points

- Organise training and data collection at one stretch. Data collection should be taken up soon after the training is conducted to minimise the time gap. This implies that ARP is to be planned at a time when the people, and the organisations are relatively free, i.e., in South India, this period could be April to June. During the agricultural season (July to December), agricultural labourers and cultivators are busy with their work. Similarly, during February and March the NGO staff are busy with annual closing of accounts and writing of reports.
- After explaining the objectives, activities and expected outcome of ARP, spend one day in explaining the concepts of poverty and local organisations.
- The discussion on the concepts of poverty and local organisations should be built on the existing knowledge of the participants (Boxes 3.2 and 3.3).
- Relate the conceptual discussion on poverty and local organisations with the methodology by asking leading questions such as which methods are most suitable to enable people to jointly analyse poverty and local organisation, and prepare action plans. If they mention PRA techniques, discuss them thoroughly.
- After providing a brief description, demonstrate how each of the methods is actually conducted. Explain also the purpose and output of the exercises. It is important to relate each of the exercises with conceptual discussion on poverty.
- While the demonstrations on PRA methods are going on, keep building a list of 'dos' and 'don'ts' on one side of the blackboard.

Box 3.2 : Initiating a discussion on poverty concepts

Begin with a question on, 'What do the participants think poverty is?' The most probable reply will be lack of basic necessities such as food, clothing and shelter. Pose them a question that 'if a household has access to food temporarily, is it out of poverty'. The participants are most likely to bring the vulnerability dimension. Slowly, enable them to bring non-material deprivation (such as vulnerability, isolation and powerlessness) into discussion.

In the second part, ask them, 'who are poor in their villages?' They are most likely to come up with an answer that households belonging to *dalits*, tribals and backward castes are the poor. Direct the discussion on to the gender dimension of poverty.

Enable the participants to have a discussion on, 'why are they poor?' This will be the most difficult part for them as they will get confused between causes and symptoms of poverty. Hence, collect all the factors that they mention without making a distinction. Then, show how 'causes' are different from 'symptoms'. Take 'lack of land' as cause of poverty, and 'disability' as symptom to drive the point.

Finally, initiate a discussion on poverty alleviation strategies of the poor. The participants are most likely to come up with individual strategies such as wage labour and undertaking IGAs, and may not bring 'collective' strategies. Try to make a distinction between 'Political' strategies (i.e., those having an impact on structural causes of poverty such as powerlessness) and individual strategies (those having impact only on individual household's income). Also make a distinction between negative strategies (migration, beedi rolling) and positive strategies (milch animal, leasing in land).

The entire discussion may take 3-4 hours of time depending on the moderation skills. The participants are more likely to relate to the discussion if the deliberations take place around one or two case studies that they themselves come up with.

Avoid giving 'definitions'. Instead, write 'key words' on a chart to give some idea on what was being discussed and come back to the chart during the remaining process of data collection, analysis and action plan preparation. If needed, an attempt can be made at the end to arrive at definitions.

Box 3.3: Initiating a discussion on local organisations involved in poverty alleviation.

Ask the participants to list the organisations in the locality. From the list, ask them to identify the organisations involved in poverty alleviation. As most of the people do not think that organisations like gram panchayats and co-operatives have anything to do with poverty, there is a tendency to exclude them. One must be careful to include all the organisations connected with poverty alleviation, even if the contribution of these local organisations to poverty alleviation is insignificant. Also enable them to include informal organisations such as SHGs and chit funds. Encourage the participants to prepare their own criteria to assess these organisations. From various factors that they bring, enable them to prepare a list consisting of accountability, efficiency, poverty commitment, and transparency and help them assess an organisation.

Acquiring Knowledge

During this phase, data on magnitude and causes of poverty, and strategies adopted by the local organisations and the poor themselves to come out of poverty were collected through the following methods.

Social Mapping

This method, which was used as an entry point into the village, aimed to map the utilisation pattern of resources available to the villagers such as housing and other infrastructural facilities (sanitation, water, electricity, school, child-care centre, PHC, bank, co-operative etc.). The purpose was also to map other characteristics such as female-headed households, handicapped, educated girls and boys, widows and child labour. This exercise was undertaken with all the people in a locality or a village.

Process Adopted

The ARP team visited the selected villages (on the day of appointment made with the villagers earlier), and encouraged the people to draw a map of the village with the help of *rangoli* powder supplied to them by the team. The villagers were encouraged to use different places such as school premises, pathway and the courtyard of a house (Box 3.4).

Box 3.4 : Conducting social mapping

Requirements

- A team of three persons should conduct the exercise: one to facilitate the exercise, one to immediately copy the information on to a chart including the legend and, another to support the process. The last person can explain the purpose, utility and end-use of exercises to curious onlookers.
- *Rangoli* powder of different colours can be used to draw the map of roads, houses and different facilities
- Charts, brown sheets, small cards and colour pens to transfer the information collected on to charts and brown sheets.
- Emergency lights if the exercises are conducted during the night-time.

Find out

- the most convenient time for the villagers;
- the village size since, in large villages, it may be necessary to conduct social mapping in two-three localities and make the combined map later; and
- a place to conduct social mapping. The school premises is good if the mapping is done during the night or on a holiday. The courtyard of a house is good if the household is acceptable to all. To the extent possible, avoid pathways.

Steps

- Go to each of the household and invite the woman/man of the household for a meeting.
- When about 20 people from the locality are present in the meeting, explain the purpose, utility and end-use of the exercise.
- Encourage someone from the group to start drawing the main road, and locate important facilities.
- Once this is complete, encourage those present to draw their own house (whether it is non-durable, semi-durable and durable) and other social characteristics.
- Encourage them to use locally available material such as seeds and different types of stones to give details on the number of children, school or non-school going children, etc.
- Copy the data immediately on to a chart, and cards.

Outcome

- Each of the villages produced a map with available resources and facilities, which provided a view that was not available to them before.
- The map helped the villagers to realise the magnitude of the problems, such as the presence of child labour, low enrolment rates among girls, sanitation and where the facilities were concentrated.
- The social maps provided initial ideas relating to the situation of the poor in the villages. They also provided clues to the questions such as: 'Who are the poor?' 'Where are they located?' 'What type of poverty do they have?'

Problems Encountered

The social mapping was different from the rest of the methods in two respects: first, it was the initial exercise conducted by the team and also done in a village. Secondly, the exercise was conducted openly. Because of these, the following problems were encountered.

- Lack of preparation not only in terms of material needed to conduct the exercise but also in terms of inability to expect different types of questions/objections/problems from the people and provide appropriate responses was a common problem.
- One of the points emphasised in the training programme was the use of locally available material (such as stones and seeds) in the mapping exercises. The team encouraged the villagers to use seeds to make a note of village characteristics. This being the first exercise in the village, the team was busy explaining the exercise to the participants, and also onlookers, and hence, did not copy down the information on to a chart paper. As it continued till midnight, the team members retired with the hope that they could continue on the following day. In the morning, all the cereals and pulses kept as legend were eaten by hens and cows and valuable information was lost! The exercise had to be redone.
- People objected to the conduct of social mapping exercise on some pretext or the other.

- In one of the villages, Muslim women refused to use *rangoli* powder as it was widely regarded as sacred powder used by the Hindus for religious and festival purposes.

Learning

- Conducting PRA methods in the NGO target villages did not mean that everyone co-operated. As some of the PRA methods were done for the entire village, one had to patiently explain the purpose, utility and the end-use.
- While conducting PRA exercises, socio-culturally accepted means and locally appropriate material were to be used.

Wealth Ranking Exercise (WRE)

Purpose

The main purpose of conducting the exercise was to: (i) know the number of poor and poorest in the villages; (ii) learn how the people themselves look at poverty, i.e. what characteristics would make a household poor, poorest, and so on; (iii) select the key informants for the remaining exercises on seasonal mapping and Focus Group Interviews; and (iv) build baseline information.

Process Adopted

The team first prepared (or obtained) a list of households either from NGO records or from electoral rolls, and wrote the names of heads of households on cards mainly to identify the households (Box 3.5). The team made an appointment with those women or men (numbering about 10-15) who could articulate on the wealth situation in the locality, and those belonging to different socio-economic groups in the locality.

The team met these key informants in a private house, school building or gram panchayat office and provided an explanation on the exercise. Subsequently, the team asked them whether the households in the locality could be classified into some wealth categories. If yes, how many categories and what should they be? Whatever the wealth categories they came up with, they were adopted. Otherwise, the team facilitated a process to enable the key informants to come up with a categorisation. The names of these categories were written on a card and kept for everybody to see. Pictures depicting different categories of the poor were drawn to help them to easily identify.

Box 3.5: Wealth ranking exercise (WRE)

Requirements

- A complete list of households in a village where ranking will be done.
- Cards with names of heads of households and identification details such as door number, surname and family name.
- A person who could draw pictures to convey the criteria evolved by the people.

Find Out

- The most convenient time for the people.
- Size of the village. The WRE can be conducted in one meeting if the village consists of less than 100 households. If it is big, conduct the exercise in homogeneous wards/localities, and in small groups. Important criterion for organising such meetings is that people need to be aware of the poverty status of other households living in their ward/locality.

Steps

- Prepare the list of households.
- Write down the names of household heads if WRE is done on the basis of household characteristics. If ranking is done with the perceptions of individuals, the names of individuals are to be written.
- Conduct the meeting in a private and/or closed place.
- Explain that the purpose of the WRE is to have a better understanding of the society, and initiate appropriate programmes for the development of the poor.
- When people come up with categories on the cards, use stones or other devices so that the categories become clear to the people present. Place the cards in front of them.
- Read out the names on cards and place them where people want them. Do not push them to arrive at a judgement. Allow them to think about the placement of cards. Ask whether everyone present agrees with the placement.
- Ask the people to count the number of cards in each category. Write down the initial count.
- After all the cards are placed, request them to come up with reasons

(Contd.)

for ranking the households (Box 3.6). One facilitator should ask the reasons for categorisation, and the other should take down the notes.

- When providing reasons for categorising the households in each category, prepare pictures relating to reasons.
- Place the pictures relating to reasons in front of them. Then ask the people whether they like to reconsider the placement of cards.
- After revisiting the cards, request the people to count them once again. Write down the revised count.
- Answer any questions relating to the exercise and purpose.
- Through all this, remember to be a friend.

One of the key informants was asked to read out the names, while others were encouraged to point out to which category the household belonged. In most of the cases, the decision was easily arrived at; but, categorisation of a few households was not easy, and resulted in a debate among the key informants. Whenever there was controversy between two persons on whether a particular household was poor or poorest, they were encouraged to keep the card between these two categories and were requested to have a second look.

After the categorisation, one of the key informants was encouraged to count the number of cards in each category. Then, they were asked to share the criteria adopted in the categorisation. The key informants, until then, had some criteria at the back of their minds and this was gradually shared with others. The team made a note of these criteria, and tried to put the criteria in the form of 'images' or 'pictures'. At the end, the team members read out the criteria and/or showed the pictures to get their confirmation (see Box 3.6, for a checklist).

When the key informants confirmed the criteria, the team proceeded further by requesting them to have a second look at the cards. This time, one of the team members read out the name on each card, and asked them whether the card should remain where it was or whether it should be shifted to another category. The key informants were encouraged to come up with the reasoning for either of the options and were requested to justify this. The team quickly wrote down these details on the back of the card. The details were, assets (land, house, livestock, etc.), education (number of children going to school, and which type of school), employment and unemployment, government assistance, number of salary earners, number of consumers to workers, etc. This became the baseline data.

Box 3.6: Checklist for the criteria on categorisation

Note that one should not prompt the people with the following. After obtaining their reasons for placing the cards, one may remind them if they have not covered any of the following points. If members mention factors other than those mentioned below, they should be welcomed.

- Female-headed or male-headed households.
- Food availability in a year (Are members in a household able to secure three meals all through the year?)
- Whether the household has higher number of children and dependants (including the disabled).
- Number of adult working members. Are children forced to work in agriculture or non-agriculture?
- Employment availability (yearly, seasonal, casual or permanent).
- Ownership of land and type of land owned (irrigated, dry, cultivable waste, *patta* land, *poromboke* land, etc.)
- Income of the household.
- Type of house (hut, thatched roof or concrete house with *pucca* roof). Whether the house is non-durable, semi-durable or durable.
- Indebtedness
- Type of jewellery.
- Are women working as agricultural labourers or in any non-agricultural work?
- Are people with illness treated in the local hospital first or city hospital first?
- Savings habit: Are savings useful to tide over difficult times during rainy season?
- Do they send children (male and female) to school?
- Ownership of productive and consumable assets.
- Clothing: Do they have only one pair or several pairs?
- Availability of ration card and whether the card is mortgaged.

After the re-classification was complete, the team encouraged one of them to count the number of cards in each of the categories, and made a note of the cards in each category during the second round. Further, the key informants were encouraged to mark these households on the resource map prepared earlier. The key informants were then asked to analyse this information. After the analysis was complete, the team shared the information on what would be the rest of the exercises with them, and thanked the respondents.

Outcome

- At the end, the team had a list of households categorised into different wealth groups (i.e., the magnitude of poverty in the village).
- The team could have a list of criteria to categorise the people into very poor, poor, better off and well off. The criteria was useful not only to understand the poverty generating processes in the village but also as a method to categorise the people in any other village.
- The method also provided some idea to the team on what aspects they should concentrate in their remaining exercises with the people. In other words, the team already obtained ideas on dimensions and causes of poverty.
- The team also had baseline information, the basis on which the impact of future interventions (if any) would be assessed.
- The community would come to know 'who were the poor in their village', and why 'they were poor'. In other words, the WRE made the people start thinking in terms of the poverty generating processes in the village.

Problems

- Since conducting one WRE for a large village was difficult, locality-wise exercises were done. In such a case, aggregating the data for the entire village was difficult.
- Quarrels arose between two key informants with regard to placing of cards in a particular category. These quarrels took place mainly because some of them thought that WRE was being done to select beneficiaries for a government programme.
- The WRE raised expectations among the people. In those cases where there was a delay between the exercises, the expectations persisted, and had a negative impact on the process.

Learning

- The facilitator has to play a crucial role even in those villages where the NGO had been working for a long period to avoid raising of expectations.
- Do not compare the results of WRE from one locality with that of the other as this might lead to wrong conclusions. For instance, the poorest from the SC locality were different from those in the upper caste locality as the yardstick used was different across the localities.

Seasonality Mapping

This exercise mapped a seasonal pattern of employment and wages, disparities in employment and wages of men and women, savings, expenditure, credit and diseases in a year. The main purpose of the exercise was to understand the severity and depth of poverty in a locality.

Process Adopted

The team made an appointment with a small group of male and female agricultural labourers and employers. The team could find who among the villagers were agricultural labourers and employers from the WRE. Key informants were encouraged to map month-wise variations in employment, unemployment, wages, expenditure (on account of known and unknown factors) and credit needed. They were also encouraged to locate the months in which the household members went without food and in such cases who among the household members were the most affected.

Outcome

- The data on severity and depth of poverty in the villages were obtained.
- The information on employment opportunities in the village, gender differences in employment availability and wages, seasonal variations in the outbreak of diseases, savings potential and expenditure was obtained.
- It became possible to decide the savings amount, seasonal variations in credit requirement, repayment schedule and amount and if and when a micro-finance programme started in the village.

Problems

- In large villages, seasonality mapping was done in 3-4 localities. Since the months used by Muslims and Hindus in seasonality mapping were different, aggregation of data for all the localities proved to be difficult.

Focus Group Interviews

In all the villages, interviews were conducted with focus groups, i.e. the poor and poorest belonging to the *dalit* community, the Muslim community and others. These interviews were conducted to enable the focus groups to map:

- relative importance of local organisations (both state and non-state) for the poor to come out of poverty;
- future strategies that the poor would like to adopt to come out of poverty;
- causes of poverty, and enabling them to rank the causes; and
- poverty alleviation strategies (individual, collective and political) adopted by the poor;

The purpose of conducting the focus group interviews was to know the causes of poverty. The mapping on poverty alleviation strategies adopted both by the poor and local organisations was done to analyse the pros and cons of strategies for future replication. The objective was also to understand the strategies that the poor would like to adopt in the future, and to prepare the ground for an action plan to alleviate poverty.

Process Adopted

In all the villages, the focus groups were selected from the data on socio-economic status collected through the WRE. Care was taken to ensure that at least a few of the persons participated in WRE and seasonality mapping for the sake of continuity. It was sought to find out whether they would be in a position to spend about 2-3 hours with the team.

On the day of appointment, the team met the focus group and explained the purpose. The exercise began with the display of pictorial information on wealth ranking and seasonality. The focus groups were asked to analyse the information. After the analysis was complete, they were asked to list the causes of poverty. Whenever the focus groups mentioned the symptoms as causes, there was discussion to make a distinction between these two, and the causes were listed in the cards. The focus groups were then asked to rank the causes of poverty. This information was written on a chart and displayed in the room itself.

The focus groups were then asked to list the strategies that they adopted to come out of poverty. Whichever strategy was mentioned, the team simply transferred it on to a chart. When the focus group did not mention about collective and political strategies, the team members tried to lead the informants to divulge information on these strategies. The team members provided some pictorial representation of the strategies mentioned, and encouraged the informants to rank them.

Subsequently, the informants were asked to list the strategies that they would like to adopt to come out of poverty, and rank these strategies. If the informants provided only individual strategies, the discussion was continued to find out whether the people would like to adopt any collective and political strategies. After encouraging them to analyse the information, brainstorming on future strategies was done to include the same in the action plans.

Output

- The team had information on causes of poverty, poverty alleviation strategies adopted by the poor and local organisations, and strategies that they would like to adopt in the future.
- This information helped the team to see whether there was continuity in terms of linkages between magnitude and causes of poverty on the one hand, and past and future strategies of the poor and local organisations on the other.
- This information was helpful to the team to have some idea on the likely action plans for the village or for a particular group.

Problems

The team found this exercise to be difficult because all the people did not participate in the exercise. Subsequently, the ranking by one articulate person became the ranking of the entire group in one or two cases.

Triangulation Exercises

Additional information from the households needed to authenticate the data were collected from the households. Further, since expectations might have influenced the results of WRE and causes of poverty, the following additional exercises needed to be conducted.

- Time related mapping to trace the important socio-economic changes in a village was done with two or three elders in each of the villages. The yardstick used to recall the changes (in irrigation facilities, crops grown, employment opportunities, infrastructure, land values, health and education facilities) was different in each case. Some used important events in their lives (such as birth of a child). Some used their age (i.e., when the person was 15 years old, 28 years old). One person used different political rules (such as Congress rule, etc.). In these exercises, PRA techniques were used to facilitate the respondent to recall the changes, and quantify the extent of change.
- Collection of primary data by canvassing a questionnaire to crosscheck the information obtained from PRA exercises. This focused upon the contribution of NGO programmes on poverty alleviation.
- Collection of data (on loans and assistance received) from government offices and banks to crosscheck the information on mapping of local organisations. This information was also useful to build the capacity of the poor with regard to what exactly they were getting from the government. Though this information was useful to triangulate the PRA exercises, the NGO team was not positively inclined towards these exercises, as it took a long time to collect and analyse the data.

Knowledge into Action

After data collection, action plans were prepared for the entire village or only for the poor. The ARP mainly focused on the preparation and presentation of action plans at the level of village and block (sub-district) levels. The NGO from Andhra Pradesh has been preparing action plans for a large number of SHGs in the district in collaboration with other NGOs.

Village Level Action Plan

Purpose

The main purpose was to bring different village level development actors together to prepare an action plan aimed at initiating, implementing and monitoring the poverty alleviation efforts. This exercise was conducted with members and leaders of SHGs, elected leaders of gram panchayats, village level officials and bankers in one-day workshop. In Tamil Nadu villages, traditional leaders attended the meetings as the system of traditional leadership is still in practice there.

Process

The process adopted in Andhra villages was different from that in Tamil Nadu villages in the sense that the action plan preparation in the former took care of the problems noticed in the latter. Hence, the process adopted in Tamil Nadu was as follows.

Responding to the invitation by the NGO leader, traditional leaders, representatives of gram panchayats and leaders of youth associations attended a one-day workshop in each of the three villages. Of about one hundred participants in each of these workshops, 60-70 were women. The programme was conducted in two sessions. During the first session, an introduction to the ARP was given and the team presented research findings with visual aids like overhead projector and charts. The participants were invited to comment on the methodology and end-results. There was no discussion on the methodology of wealth ranking, seasonality mapping, causes of poverty and strategies that they adopted. But, a few doubts were expressed on mapping of local organisations as the participants understood the distance in geographical terms rather than in terms of poverty orientation. Barring this, the people present expressed that the information was correct and accurate.

The discussion on action plans was initiated with the focus on

causes of poverty and future strategies of the poor. The discussion initially concentrated on the identification of needs (individual and group). An effective facilitation was needed to direct the discussion towards strategies and action plans. The predominant view of the participants was that undertaking of certain income generating activities and awareness building activities was needed for the time being, and long-term strategies aimed at poverty reduction could be given thought later. The traditional leaders and elected representatives of the gram panchayats contributed considerably to the preparation of action plans.

Output

- At the end, the SHGs, together with the other development actors at the village level, developed an action plan based on the situation and needs of the poor.
- The villagers had been meeting the ARP team in small groups for data collection. They did not have much idea on what would be the end product. With an action plan emerging and other development actors present in the meeting, the interest of the people in the process was more than doubled.
- For the villagers, the workshop was the first of its kind which provided a ground for the people and elected leaders to come together in one meeting to discuss the issues relating to poverty alleviation.
- The meeting also helped the people to demand accountability from the elected representatives. In one of the villages, the poor posed a few questions to their ward member in the gram panchayat regarding whether the gram panchayat could support the activities identified and incorporated in the action plan. She was not able to answer the questions and admitted in the meeting that she was not very much aware of the panchayat activities. The participants also added that she was not a person who could decide for the panchayat nor could talk in the panchayat for the people.
- The meetings also helped to question the elected representatives with regard to their biased activities. In one of the villages in Tamil Nadu, one person alleged that the ward member was favouring his own community in the

distribution of milch cows. This resulted in considerable debate and discussion among the people who attended the meeting.

Problems

- There was a dilemma between inviting many people to improve the ownership, and inviting only a few selected villagers and important development actors in the village for a meaningful interaction. In Tamil Nadu villages, the preference was for the former, which has had its own problems. The participants' strength was quite high to begin with; but, slowly, people started to move out of the meeting, and at the end not many were left.
- The elected leaders of gram panchayats did not stay until the end. They left soon after the presentation of the results was over.
- With the number of participants being large, the workshop could not discuss the issues seriously. It became more of information sharing and brainstorming rather than preparing an action plan.
- The availability of space to conduct this kind of meeting was a problem in rural areas. The most convenient place was the school building. But with school functioning during the entire week, the workshop had to be conducted only on Sunday. Also getting the village-level officials on Sundays was difficult.
- The meeting was conducted in the village itself as it was felt that this would be convenient to a large proportion of the people, including men and women. But, conducting a large meeting created another kind of problem, namely, people could not sit in the meeting, and they kept going and coming.

Learning

- It is important to develop a draft action plan in the small meetings and present the same in the larger ones as it was difficult to involve people to prepare the action plan in large meetings. In any case, the villagers may not be in a position to spend so much of time for the meeting. This can be done after the villagers develop the capacity to prepare action plans on their own.

- There is a need to prepare very well for the workshop.
- All the development actors, including government officials and bankers at the village level are to be involved in the meeting.
- The people normally come up with only activities resulting in individual benefits. They may not come up with strategies or any action plan having significant impact on the structures prevailing at the village level. Hence, this needs to be taken up as a continuous process.

Block Level Action Plan

Workshops were conducted at the block level involving people from selected villages and block level officials (elected leaders of gram panchayats, bankers, leaders and members of SHGs, traditional leaders, the poor and ARP team from the NGO) to strengthen the action plans developed at the village level. The second objective was to share the information, obtain feedback from the concerned officials, and commitment for resources, if needed. And, finally, to lobby and advocate the utility of ARP and the need to look at the problem holistically and bring various actors together for sustainable poverty alleviation.

The Process Adopted

The workshop, to develop block level plans, was conducted for three days, each day meant for one village. Everyday, the meeting began with a welcome and a brief introduction to ARP given by the NGO. This was followed by the presentation of results by the ARP team members and presentation of action plan by the leaders of SHGs. The visual aids like OHP and charts were used in the presentation. The officials sought a few clarifications on the methodology and results. For instance, one official asked why data on four categories of people were presented when the focus was only on the poor.

In the afternoon, the participants were divided into 3-5 groups for discussion on the action plan. Each of the groups reworked the action plans prepared at the village level and added new activities to the list. The final output contained far more detailed information on resources and how to go about acquiring the same. The group reports were presented in the plenary, and all the participants provided comments on action plans.

Lack of close relationship between causes and action plan caught the attention of one or two officials. Similarly, the action plans reflected the individual strategies, and not political strategies. It was noted in the workshop that there was need to think of political strategies once the immediate needs of the poor were met.

Output

- At the end, the SHGs, elected representatives to gram panchayats, officials and ARP team had an action plan to be implemented in a time-bound manner.
- Helped the different actors to come together on a single platform. The ARP data, which conveyed certain scientific look, objectivity and seriousness, helped the officials to make up their minds with regard to the implementation.
- Convergence between people's needs and programmes of different development actors (government departments, banks, gram panchayats and co-operatives) could be achieved.
- Higher acceptance of SHGs by the officials.
- Helped further the linkages between SHGs and government departments.

Problems

- People gave priority to only programmes that benefited them individually.
- People did not think of those actions which would have an impact on structural aspects conditioning poverty. For instance, neither the people nor the team thought that it was their right to access the resources, and that there should be concrete action plan towards achieving that goal.
- The follow-up of action plans suffered because it was felt that the ARP team should take a lead in monitoring the action plans. In the context of problems discussed with the team, this meant that there was no effective monitoring of the action plans.

Conclusions

The ARP provided valuable inputs to those organisations, which wanted to become learning ones. It also enabled the project initiators to understand the situation of the poor, their needs, and prepare an action plan to alleviate poverty based on situation and needs. For poverty reduction to take place, the process of learning, action, and reflection should become an integral part of an organisation. It was not sufficient if this was taken as a one-time project and the follow-up was not adequate.

The PRA techniques were particularly helpful to enable people's participation. But, there were limitations such as longer time needed if the exercise was to be conducted in larger number of villages and difference between these methods and survey. The survey would capture the views of several people on what strategies needed to be adopted, while the same might not be possible in PRA exercises if effective facilitation was not done. Thus, there was trade-off between survey and PRA when the exercises were to be conducted in a larger number of villages. This could be sorted out by conducting social mapping, WRE, seasonality mapping and focus group interviews, and canvassing a short questionnaire on strategies and local organisations. The difference between the results of the survey and PRA could be sorted out with the help of a daily review of the process.

There was a danger that the needs-analysis might result in coming up with a shopping list and that people might show preference to poverty alleviation rather than poverty reduction. It was also possible that the poor might come up with individual strategies aimed at their survival and security. They might not come up with the political strategies that had influence on the structures that perpetuated inequality and that generated poverty. Hence, this aspect needed to be borne in mind from the beginning, and effective facilitation assuming importance.

For significant and sustainable impact on poverty reduction, situation analysis, needs assessment and preparation of action plan should become an integral of the intervention process adopted by an organisation. Where this was difficult, there was a need to collaborate with Gram Panchayats which were also supposed to prepare area plans based on the methodology outlined in this chapter. If these two actors could come together in this area of action research, the benefits to the community would be enormous.

4

An Analysis of Poverty in the Selected Villages

Introduction

What have been the processes that generated poverty in the selected villages? Were there changes in the socio-economic status of the different sections in the villages? If yes, what were they and how did they occur? Were there any changes in the magnitude and condition of poverty? An analysis of these questions is important because these are the processes which influence the space available for development actors to alleviate poverty. It is the analysis of these questions which suggests the local organisations whether there is need for new and innovative intervention strategies. It is this analysis which provides ideas relating to the need for a particular resource, a particular possibility for the poor, etc. It is this analysis which connects the local with macro, and enable the poor to see the root causes of their local problems in macro policies and programmes, and this, in turn, enables them to seek to influence the policies and programmes conceived and implemented by the state. This chapter, therefore, analyses the changes in the socio-economic status of the different sections in the villages and processes that generated poverty in the study area.

Poverty: Processes, Situation and Magnitude in Tamil Nadu Villages

Historical Processes

Time related mapping[1] was done in all the villages to trace the important socio-economic changes in the villages. The results of the mapping were similar to the resurveys conducted in 11 villages very close to the selected villages. Earlier, a survey was conducted by the Cambridge University, U.K. and Madras University, Madras, in 1973-74, the results of which were published in *Farmer* (1977). Ten years later, a second survey (Hazell and Ramasamy 1993) was conducted by the International Food Policy Research Institute (IFPRI) and Tamil Nadu Agricultural University (TNAU). The third survey was conducted as part of a research project on Adjustment and Development: Agrarian Change, Markets and Social Welfare in South India, 1973-93. An article on important findings was published by Harris-White and Janakarajan (1997). This section is based on the results of mapping exercises on socio-economic changes in the villages as well as on the results of these surveys.

Around 1950s, the agricultural population in these villages protected themselves against scanty and uncertain rainfall and droughts with tank irrigation. In all the villages, tanks were collectively maintained and were used to recharge wells. Fields were irrigated through water drawn from wells either through human *(etram)* or animal *(kavalai)* power[3]. Much of the area was irrigated by tanks and wells[4]. All the land in the villages was cultivated and the important crops were paddy, ragi and groundnut. Agriculture was the main source of employment as water lifting and cultivation were done with human and animal power. The wages paid were low around Rs. 2 per day; but agricultural labourers led a decent life. The purchasing power was stated to be high and health status was good as the diet consisted of locally grown staple foodgrains and pulses. In all the villages, the main caste groups were Vanniyars and Scheduled Castes (SCs). But, there were also Mudaliars in Melvallam, Potters in Mottupalyam and Muslims in Sabthalipuram. The SC households lived in their own hamlet away from the main village, and caste discrimination was prevalent. The villagers cited incidents of 'persons from depressed castes walking away without shoes in the upper caste locality'; 'the lower caste people moving a few yards away when the upper caste person was passing by'.

From late 1950s and 1960s, farmers started constructing wells in the command area (and also non-command area) of tanks following a widespread drought in early 1960s. The number of wells in the district increased from 1.5 lakhs in 1950 to 1.75 lakhs in 1960.

Subsequently, well irrigation gained prominence at the expense of tank irrigation[5] and the number of diesel engines increased. This, however, did not have any dramatic impact on employment because the growth of diesel engines was slow[6], and water lifting and cultivation were still done with human and animal labour. The employment opportunities improved as the growth in well irrigation increased cropping intensity, and production. The employment opportunities were also stated to be better because of the coming up of a sugar mill in the vicinity of villages and quarrying.

Dramatic changes began to occur from late 1960s with the adoption of new agricultural technology in the district. The package of technology included the supply of High Yielding Varieties (HYV) of seeds, and support towards the purchase of other inputs, namely credit and fertilisers. The area under HYV paddy increased rapidly in 1960s[7]. The results of the first survey (Farmer 1977) indicate that transplanting and use of manure was widespread; fertilisers and manures were widely used; yield rates had gone up; and the cultivation of paddy had become profitable. The adoption rate increased with the size of operational holding; but, small farmers registered the highest rate of adoption as compared to marginal and rich farmers. The main constraints in not adopting and limited adoption of HYVs were inadequate credit facilities and water (Chinnappa 1977).

The farmers, interested in adopting HYVs, sought to solve the 'water problem' through expansion of well irrigation and purchase of electric pumpsets. The total number of wells in the district increased from 0.5 lakhs in 1905 to 1.51 lakhs in 1950 and to 1.75 lakhs in 1961 and to 2.29 lakhs in 1971. Thus, the fastest growth of wells took place during the period 1961-71 when over 50,000 wells were constructed in the district (Bandara 1977:325). In order to improve the efficiency of the water lifting, energisation of open wells increased at a rapid rate. The number of electric pumpsets increased from 20,000 in 1960 to 1.20 lakhs in 1973-74 (Bandara 1977:325). By mid-1970s, over 50 per cent of the wells in the district were fitted with electric pumpsets. The main reasons for a rapid diffusion of electric water lifting technology were: economical and technical superiority over the older forms, profits from the cultivation, subsidised loans and electricity provided by the government (Harris 1977).

Increased yields, production and incomes through the adoption of new agricultural technology and almost no farm mechanisation improved the employment opportunities for the poor. Notwithstanding the reduced employment opportunities on account of energisation of wells, the money wages for male farm labourers increased from Rs. 2 (with food) in late 1950s to Rs.15 (with food) in 1970s. The corresponding figures for female agricultural labourers were Rs. 0.5 and Rs. 6. There was an upward mobility of a few SC households due to adoption of HYV technology[8], improved work opportunities and salaried employment in the military.

By 1980s, there was a rapid rise in the area under HYVs, and consumption of fertilisers and pesticides. The real incomes from the cultivation of paddy and groundnut increased (Hazell and Ramasamy 1993). But, well irrigation began to have adverse consequences. Between 1971 and 1982, 71,722 wells were dug in the district taking the total number to over 3 lakhs. The villagers reported that with a rapid rise in wells and drying up of the tanks and lakes, the ground-water table kept decreasing. This necessitated large investments on deepening of wells and purchase of electric pumpsets with a higher lift power. Small farmers could not make such a high investment, and hence, went in for less water intensive crops such as groundnut and banana (Hazell and Ramasamy 1993:34). Thus, although 'water problems' were solved constraints of new type emerged.

The impact of new agricultural technology on employment was becoming negative. The villagers reported that the employment opportunities within agriculture were reduced due to mechanisation and introduction of less labour intensive crops. Labour saving technology was considered to be important because of reduced time gap between the crops on account of short maturing nature of the HYVs, and double cropping. With credit facilities provided by the banks and agrarian surplus, the wealthy farmers adopted labour saving technology (electric pumpsets, tractors, threshers, harvesters, etc.). By mid-1970s, mechanised ploughing of dry land became much more extensive. Threshing through machines had become quite common (Harris 1977: 141). "Total employment in crop production declined by 4 per cent per paddy farm in the resurvey villages between 1973-74 and 1983-84. This decline is attributable to a downward trend in labour use per hectare for both HYVs and local varieties during 1970s, a reflection of increased mechanisation of irrigation pumping and paddy threshing. The loss in per hectare paddy employment was sufficiently large ... to offset the employment gains from an increase in the paddy crop area on both small and large farms. The use of family labour increased on both small and large farms between 1973-74 and 1983-84, hence, the brunt of decline in total employment fell on the hired workers" (Hazell and Ramasamy 1993:240). Yet, real wage rates modestly increased 'because of a decline in the amount of hired labour supplied by farms operating more than one hectare of land, and because of competing employment opportunities in dairying and non-farm activities' *(ibid)*. The mapping in the selected villages show that the non-agricultural employment opportunities increased in 1980s. The introduction of labour saving technology reduced work opportunities within agriculture for the labourers belonging to the depressed castes.

By 1990s, low rainfall, reduced groundwater table and drying up of tanks resulted in the shrinkage of irrigated area and growth of cultivable wastes in the villages. About 20 years ago, Bandara (1977) concluded that "the hydro-ecological balance in North Arcot district is under strain, if not becoming rapidly upset". The fact that the strain was evidenced by the lowering water tables even during the years of high rainfall, made Bandara (1977: 337) to warn that "further expansion of lift irrigation may lead in the near future to unwelcome hydrological consequences such as lowering water tables and dwindling of surface water resources, unless suitable preventive measures are introduced in time". The spacing norms were introduced by the government; but, these seemed to be violated. Although the construction of new wells had slowed down, about 5,000 to 7,000 wells in the district were energised each year in 1980s. The rate at which wells were abandoned also increased. With the collapse of traditional water management practices on tanks and tank water getting polluted with agro-chemical effluent, the tank in Sabthalipuram was only useful to supply the silt for making bricks. Now, the villages completely depend upon well irrigation. But with competitive deepening of wells leading to high failure rate, the agricultural yields are getting affected. The paddy yield rate declined from 3.5 tonnes per hectare in 1973-74 to 3.2 tonnes per hectare in 1993-94. Groundnut yields also declined from 1.4 tonnes per hectare to 1.0 tonne per hectare during the same period (Harris-White and Janakarajan 1997).

The problems associated with well irrigation were most severe among the small and marginal farmers. They had neither sufficient capital to deepen the well nor could face the risk of failure of deepening venture. Hence, the competition for deepening was mostly among the better-off farmers. Secondly, with deepening of wells, the energy consumed per well increased from 2,501 units in 1980-81 to 3,897 units in 1992-93. This increased the costs of cultivation. Third, the power cuts often made it difficult to have required irrigation for crops like paddy. These problems resulted in cropping pattern changes especially among the small farmers. The re-surveys in 1993-94 reveal that the bulk of the area owned by small peasants was cultivated with groundnut, while rich peasants continued to grow paddy on large proportion of the area (Harris-White and Janakarajan 1997: 1473).

The employment opportunities in both the villages declined due to: (i) a decline in well irrigated area; (ii) decline in yields and production; (iii) growth of marginal farmers (due to a combination of sale and partition[9] and consequent reduction in employment as these tended to be family operated; and (iv) farm mechanisation. The farm mechanisation was a recurring theme in all the surveys. Except the initial survey, other surveys confirmed the growing farm mechanisation and a shift to less labour intensive (and income elastic) crops of bananas, vegetables, casurinas, etc. The mapping exercises revealed a rapid rise in the agricultura money wages in 1980s and 1990s which is confirmed by the resurveys. The paradox of wide-spread agricultural unemployment co-existing with rising wages could be explained by the growth of non-farm employment opportunities in the villages. Quarrying, beedi rolling, construction, commuting to Vellore town to work in the urban informal sector, trades, services, etc., became important non-agricultural employment avenues in Sabthalipuram, while construction, leather tanning, trades and services and head-load work were important in Mottupalyam and Melvallam. Both pull and push factors operated: the pull factor was higher wages in non-farm sector[10], while push factor was a worsening of employment opportunities within agriculture together with low wages.

The time related mapping also brings out qualitative changes that have taken place in the villages. With an improvement in educational facilities and the introduction of a noon-meal scheme, the educational levels in the villages have, in general, improved. The health status seems to have come down with the changes in consumption pattern and problems of sanitation (poor drainage in both the villages is leading to growth of mosquitoes), notwithstanding improved medical facilities. The resurveys on nutritional status reveal that while the nutritional intake among the better-off households vastly improved between 1973-74 and 1983-84 on account of increased yields and income, there was 70 per cent shortfall in the case of landless households (Andersen and Jaramillo 1993). By 1990s, the households with nutritional stress were estimated to be between 17-35 per cent among poor peasants and landless households (Harris-White and Janakarajan 1997: 1474).

The social status of the depressed castes improved due to their upward mobility (on account of the adoption of HYVs, improved employment opportunities within and outside agriculture). An active *dalit* movement against untouchability and temple entry restrictions in the northern Tamil Nadu also contributed to this. Now, there is free mixing of persons belonging to upper and lower castes. The upper caste persons go to the houses of depressed castes and attend marriages; but do not eat food. Harris, (1993) and Harris-White and Janakarajan (1997) bring a different dimension of discrimination when they note that there are social restrictions of entry into highly capital intensive and profitable non-farm activities, which is again confirmed by our mapping.

The foregoing discussion suggests that the changes in the lift irrigation technology and new agricultural technology led to intended consequences such as growth in the area under HYVs, increased yields, double cropping, enhanced employment opportunities, rising wages and adoption of new agricultural technology by small and marginal farmers (including those belonging to SC households). On the other hand, the changes in cropping pattern in favour of less labour intensive crops and overall decline in employment opportunities due to mechanisation were unintended consequences. The political space for the poor was influenced by both intended and unintended consequences. The problem of unemployment was due to government subsidy oriented policies aimed at water lifting technology and mechanisation within agriculture. Yet, the poor could not see this being the reason for widespread unemployment. The fact that the new agricultural technology enabled some of the poor to become better-off through individual based entrepreneurial strategies made the other poor to blame themselves for their poverty rather than pointing their fingers at the deep rooted structural factors and government policies as root causes. The analysis also shows that poverty had become more diverse and complex. Poverty was interlinked with the processes of agricultural growth and change, and access to resources. This might have come in the way of having political discourse in which poverty was a significant issue.

The Selected Villages: Condition and Severity of Poverty

There are 179 households in Sabthalipuram; of them, a majority are Vanniyars—a dominant caste in the locality. This village, located only 13 kms away from Vellore town, enjoys certain benefits such as wide-spread availability of employment in brick making, quarrying, beedi rolling, informal sector in Vellore town, etc., though agriculture is by no means unimportant. The important crops grown are paddy, groundnut and sugarcane. The facilities present are commercial bank, cooperative bank, fair price shop, gram panchayat, agricultural extension office, village development office, protected water supply, etc. (a few of these facilities are located in the neighbouring village). The village also has a craft centre and SHGs which were started by SHARE (Chart 4.1).

In Mottupalayam, there are 182 households; a majority of them are *dalits* (both SCs and cobblers). The village can be termed as predominantly agrarian because most of the households derive their sustenance from agriculture. The important crops grown are paddy, groundnut and banana. The households are involved in non-agricultural activities such as construction, trades, business, services, etc. Persons from a significant proportion of the households have found employment in the defence. The possibilities of working in urban informal sector are, however, limited. The village is also endowed with the same infrastructural facilities as that of Sabthalipuram. The NGO has started the craft centre and formed SHGs for women (Chart 4.1).

In Melvallam, there are 215 households, most of which belong to Vanniyar caste. At the time of the survey, there was conflict between the two castes on the pathway to carry dead bodies belonging to SC caste to the burial ground. The matter was often taken to the

Chart 4.1: Basic Characteristics of the villages

Particulars	Sabthalipuram	Mottupalayam	Melvallam
Type of village	13 kms away from Vellore town; hence, there is urban influence. A majority of the households depend on non-farm activities.	22 kms away from Vellore town; predominantly agricultural village though non-farm activities are also important.	20 kms away from Vellore town; predominantly agricultural.
Important caste groups	Vanniyar, Scheduled Castes (SCs) and Muslims.	Vanniyar and SCs.	Vanniyar and SCs.
Number of households	179	182	215
Facilities available	Elementary school, fair price shop, protected water supply.	Elementary school and gram panchayat.	School, balwadi, TNIP centre, community centre.
Facilities located in the neighbouring village	Bank, gram panchayat, cooperative, agricultural extension office, village development office, etc., are located in a village which is 1.5 kms away from the village.	Bank, cooperative, agricultural extension office, village development office, etc., are located in a village which is 0.5 km away from the village.	Cooperative, village development office.
Non-farm employment opportunities	Quarrying, beedi rolling, construction, brick making, shops, trades and services. Being close to Vellore, many people go to town for work.	Construction, leather tanning, brick making, shops, trades and services.	Not extensive: Some households engage in loading and unloading of sand trucks.
NGO work	Craft centre, Self-Help Groups (SHGs), children's creche, borewell.	Craft centre, SHGs, evening study centre.	None.

Source: Resource mapping in the selected villages.

police, and the SC households sought police protection whenever there was death in the community. The village is predominantly agrarian with most of the households depending on agriculture for sustenance.

Condition of Poverty

The wealth ranking[11] exercises in the selected villages provided us with the distribution of households by wealth categories (Table 4.1). The criteria adopted by the people in the wealth ranking were

Table 4.1: Distribution of households by wealth categories in Tamil Nadu villages

Categories	Distribution of households (%) by wealth categories in the colonies of Sabthalipuram			Distribution of households (%) by wealth categories in the colonies of Mottupalyam			Distribution of households (%) by wealth categories in the colonies of Melvallam	
	Vanniyar	Cobblers	Muslims	Vanniyars	Cobblers	SCs	Vanniyars	SCs
Very poor	8.7	27.5	14.9	17.8	51.5	22.4	10.5	59.1
Poor	19.6	57.5	44.7	15.1	39.4	44.7	12.9	13.0
Better-off	21.7	15.0	33.3	32.9	9.1	7.9	64.3	11.4
Well-off	50.0	0.0	11.5	34.2	0.0	25.0	12.3	12.3
Total	100.0	100.0	100.0	100.0	100.0	100.0	100.0	100.0
	(92)	(40)	(47)	(73)	(33)	(76)	(171)	(44)

Note: Figures in parentheses denote total number of households in each colony.

broad[12] and varied between Vanniyar, and Muslim and SC localities, and hence, the very poor in the SC locality were different from the same category in the Vanniyar locality. For this reason, the poverty level in one locality could be compared with that of another. Table 4.1 suggests that, in all the villages, a larger proportion of SC households were poor and very poor. In one village, a bulk of the Muslim households were poor.

The criteria adopted also show that the very poor were characterised by material deprivation, assetlessness, unemployment, casualisation of wage labour, higher dependency ratio, presence of child labourers, inability to utilise the existing educational and health facilities, and dependence on employers for consumption credit. The poor had similar characteristics; but, the main difference between poor and very poor was that while the former were characterised by relatively lower dependency ratio, the presence of family members in the working age, and hence, were able to access the employment opportunities in the agricultural and non-agricultural sectors, the poorest were handicapped in this regard. Though the poor suffered from the problem of uncertain employment in the rainy season, the savings from earnings during the peak season came to their rescue during the off-season. Further, the poor, though they did not have serious livelihood problems, suffered from vulnerability as they did not possess the assets and/or suffered from the inability to obtain regular employment. The well-off and better-off households not only possessed productive assets and were involved in non-farm activities (as owners), but also had access to government and other benefits, and had household members with salaried employment. The well-off among SC households were characterised by members with salaried employment, better educational levels, participation in local decentralised government, good networks with government institutions, etc.

Severity of Poverty

Seasonality mapping[13] and focus group interviews[14] with the poor and poorest in three localities of each village and open-ended interviews with 10 per cent of the very poor and poor households formed the data base for the following discussion on severity of poverty. The severity of poverty was different across the villages and between men and women as the livelihood opportunities differed.

First, there were differences across the villages in the source of employment. In Sabthalipuram, non-farm activities formed an important source of employment and livelihood, while agriculture was the important source of employment in Mottupalyam and Melvallam. Since agricultural employment tended to be seasonal, work opportunities were less in Mottupalyam and Melvallam where male workers had full employment for four months, 10 days of employment in another four months and occasional employment in the remaining months. In contrast, male workers in Sabthalipuram had full employment in five months, 15 days of employment in another two months and 10 days of employment in five months.

There were also gender differences in this. In Sabthalipuram, while male workers found non-farm employment in quarrying, construction, brick factories in the vicinity of the village and informal sector in Vellore town, women were involved in both non-farm (beedi rolling and NGO craft centre) and farm activities. In Mottupalyam, while most of the men were involved in non-farm activities of construction, leatherwork, and small business, female workers were mainly involved in agriculture. The pattern in Melvallam was similar to Mottupalyam except that some of the women in the latter village worked in the NGO craft centre. This had implications as far as the availability of employment for men and women. Male workers had better employment opportunities in Sabthalipuram. In Mottupalyam and Melvallam, female workers had employment all through the year while male workers had very little employment in four months. But the employment opportunities, which were highly seasonal, reached the peak both in agriculture and non-agriculture during the harvesting season, and were very low during the rainy and summer seasons. The quarrying came to a halt during the rainy season; so also, the work in the craft centre and beedi rolling as the quality of the work got affected due to dampness of the palm and beedi leaves.

The wage rates also varied depending on the source of the employment. The daily wage rates were Rs. 25-30 for men and Rs. 20 for women (without food) for agricultural work during the peak season. During the slack season, wage rates did not decline; but, the number of working hours seemed to be longer. In quarrying, men received Rs. 60 per day, while women received Rs. 30 per day. Beedi workers earned Rs. 30 for rolling 1,000 beedies. In construction, daily wage rates went up to Rs. 80.

The wage rates were thus high for quarrying and construction. Yet, not all the workers could participate in these activities. Quarrying in Sabthalipuram was mostly confined to men in the Muslim and SC households because this work involved loading and unloading of the trucks. Hence, women (especially Muslim women) did not prefer to participate in them. There was also fear of high accident rate. In Sabthalipuram, bread-earning members from three poor households became physically handicapped in accidents, and as a result, these households slid into the category of the poorest. Similarly, beedi rolling was almost restricted to the households of physically weak men, and Muslims.

There was gender division as far as the work opportunities were concerned. A larger proportion of the women were engaged in agriculture[15] because of two reasons; landlords preferred women workers as wage rates for them were lower, and men preferred to work in highly paid non-farm activities. Due to *pardah* system[16], unmarried girls and young women did not take part in agricultural work. Hence, they were mainly involved in beedi rolling, craft centre, etc. The poor households belonging to non-SC communities perceived that the work in the craft centre was of low status. All these factors constrained women's access to highly paid non-farm employment, and forced them to take up disease-prone beedi rolling and low paying agricultural work.

The incidence of common diseases was also high during the rainy season. As a result, the intensity of food shortages was much more during the rainy season. The Muslims also faced difficulties during Ramzan month as the festival expenditure went up[17], and the ability to work declined due to fasting. The non-Muslims also faced shortages during those festivals which occurred during the off-season. In both rainy season, and festival months, the poorest met the basic needs through loans borrowed from financiers and moneylenders at high interest rates. These got accumulated if the households did not clear them off in the peak season owing to reasons such as illness of principal earning member and sudden decline in the employment opportunities as a result of drought. In this respect, the poor were better in the sense that the lower dependency ratio (of consumers to workers) enabled them to have savings which could be drawn during the slack season, and hence, their dependence on moneylenders was relatively less.

On account of less employment opportunities during the rainy season, many of the poorest households could only afford two meals. Food shortage was acute among female-headed households, and also with those with physically handicapped as heads of households. When there was shortage of food, the men and male children were given priority. Among Muslim households, there was no discrimination against aged and female children. Among SC households, aged were discriminated in food allocation. In all the localities, it was the women who got the least priority during the periods of food shortages.

Causes of Poverty

In focus group interviews conducted in seven localities across the selected villages, the poor and poorest households were asked to list and rank the causes of poverty. The causes of poverty overlapped, and were mixed up with symptoms of poverty. Sen's framework on causes of poverty is useful in this context. According to Sen (1981), failures relating to endowment (assetlessness, physical weakness and lack of citizenship), production (quality of the assets, lack of education and skills and lack of help from the government) and exchange (prices of produce, unemployment and wages) resulted in poverty. Kabeer (1996) includes consumption (intra-household inequality, vices such as drinking, higher dependency ratio, etc.) failures as another cause of poverty.

Table 4.2 shows that higher dependency ratio (i.e., consumers to workers ratio) was cited as the cause in all the localities, while assetlessness, unemployment and vices were cited as causes in six out of seven localities. Lack of education and skills, and physical weakness were cited in five out of seven localities. As most of the very poor and poor households did not have land or other productive assets, they had to hire themselves out in either agriculture or non-agriculture. But, widespread unemployment, which was cited as a cause of poverty in six out of seven localities, came in the way of obtaining livelihood. It was perceived that lack of employment opportunities especially in non-farm sector was due to lack of education and skills. Another reason for not exploiting the employment opportunities within agriculture was physical weakness which was mainly due to illness, lack of adequate diet, inability to access health care facilities. Even if some of the households managed to obtain employment, the wage income was not sufficient because of higher dependency ratio. The 'bad habits' such as drinking was cited as a cause for poverty in six localities (mostly SC and Muslim) as male workers spent most of their earnings on drinking and this caused consumption failures within the households.

Table 4.2 : Causes of poverty in the selected villages

Causes of poverty	Number of localities where the cause is cited
Lack of assets	6
Unemployment	6
Physical weakness	5
Lack of education and skills	5
Higher dependency ratio	7
Vices (drinking, etc.)	6
Lack of help from the government	3
Low wages	2
Female headed households	3

The analysis on the condition and severity of poverty together with historical processes generating poverty suggested that relative poverty between the poor and the well-off and also within the SC households seemed to have increased. The new agricultural technology together with non-farm activities and salaried employment helped the well-off households as well as some of the SC households to prosper in the last three decades or so. At the same time, the very poor in the 1950s also experienced economic mobility due to improved employment opportunities. The discussion also suggests that land as the principal source of livelihood opportunities lost some of its importance both for labourers and cultivators. Further, the nature of livelihood options differed across the villages, and also between men and women; so also, the condition and severity of poverty.

Processes, Situation and Magnitude of Poverty in Andhra Villages

Krishna district, where the selected villages are located, can be divided into two parts—eastern and western. The eastern part benefited from a barrage constructed across the river Krishna about 150 years ago.

Following the construction, there was a process of commercialisation of agriculture with paddy becoming an important commercial crop triggering development in land, credit and labour markets in the last half of the nineteenth century (Rao 1985). The first half of this century witnessed an intensification of commercialised agriculture accompanied by development of agro-processing industries (Rao and Rajasekhar 1991). The new agricultural technology was introduced in the eastern part of the district from the mid-1960s and consequently, the traditional varieties of paddy were replaced by the high yielding ones.

In contrast, the western part of the district is located in upland areas where irrigation was not developed and cultivation of dry crops was predominant. Nevertheless, this part also witnessed an intensive commercialisation of agriculture centred around tobacco, cotton, chillies and groundnut (Rao 1985) with imperial capital showing considerable interest in the first crop (Duvvury 1999). This process of commercialisation continued up to the independence and even after; but, the productivity of agriculture and the degree of commercialisation were much less in the western part as compared to the eastern part. The provision of irrigation through the Nagarjuna Sagar Dam in the mid-1960s enabled the farmers in a few taluks to go in for paddy cultivation and new agricultural technology.

Socio-economic Changes in Andhra Villages

The discussion with three key informants in each of the villages formed the database for documenting the socio-economic changes in these villages. The reference point used by the key informants was different in each case. However, each one of them discussed the changes between 1950 and 1998, and hence, the period could be divided as 1950 to 1965, 1966 to 1980 and post-1980.

The Period of 1950 to 1965

The total area under irrigation was less in the villages. Hence, most of the land was rainfed. The groundwater table was good. According to one of the informants, all that they had to do was to dig 5 to 10 feet for obtaining groundwater. Yet, the area cultivated by wells was negligible.

Mostly dry crops such as jowar, variga, korra, cotton and

groundnut were cultivated. Only farm manure was used. Pesticides were not used at all. The system of attached labour was prominent. The attached labourers worked with a farmer throughout the year, and were paid both in cash and kind. In addition, the employer provided food and shelter. Casual wage labour was also prevalent, and the wages paid to men and women were Rs. 2 to 3 (or 5 kgs of grain) and Rs.1 to 1.50, respectively, per day.

There was gender-based division of labour. Men were ploughing and preparing the soil for cultivation, while women were engaged in weeding and plucking of green gram. Children were not engaged in agricultural work due to less work and less demand. In fact, the farmers did not allow the children to work. Migration was essentially confined to a couple of households in the village.

The value of one acre of land ranged from Rs.1,000 to Rs.1,500 depending on the type of soil. The lease market was not very well developed. Fixed tenancy was practised, and the farmers were expecting Rs. 50 for leasing out of one acre of land. Half of the amount was usually given as advance. This barred the poor from leasing in the land.

Mostly Brahmins were educated, and were teachers in village schools. The prevalence of caste system and untouchability came in the way of education of children belonging to SC households. Mostly, traditional and home-made medicines were used for all types of illnesses. The market orientation was limited. The government support was restricted to distribution of inferior cereals through the public distribution system, which was not, in any case, popular with the poor households.

The Period 1966 to 1980

Two important changes in the endowment of the poor households could be noticed during this period. First, the government distributed land under land reforms programme. A few of the poor households also came to possess land through a combined process of cultivation of waste lands and purchasing land in the market owing to gradual migration of the landed households from the villages. Second, the government provided housing facility to the SC households. In Bathinapadu villages, 54 households were provided with housing facility on condition that each one of them contributed Rs.1,100.

However, 14 poorest households could not contribute this amount, and hence, could not avail this facility.

There were changes in irrigation. Slowly, well irrigation became predominant in Bathinapadu [where water was lifted from the Krishna river and canals (located at some distance) through oil engines], and canal irrigation in Kothapeta due to the construction of Nagarjuna Sagar Dam. The availability of irrigation water resulted in changes in the cropping pattern in favour of commercial crops such as paddy, cotton, groundnut, red gram and tobacco. The farmers began to use fertilisers and pesticides. The chemical agriculture got intensified by the end of this period. The value of one acre of land increased to Rs.20,000 to 25,000. The lease value per acre also increased to Rs.1,000 to 1,500. The entire amount had to be paid in advance.

The wage labour market witnessed a few important changes. First, while the system of attached labourer (who was paid Rs. 1,000 to 2,000 per year besides food and clothing) continued, the wage labour market was getting casualised at a rapid rate. Second, men continued to be involved in ploughing and preparation of land. However, tractor technology reduced employment opportunities for men. Hence, they were involved in plucking of tobacco leaf, harvesting of paddy, groundnut, red gram, etc. The employment opportunity for women in the form of weeding and transplantation remained intact, and in fact, improved with the emergence of labour intensive crops such as cotton and tobacco. Third, due to heavy demand for wage labour, the children were gradually getting involved in agricultural labour market, and were paid wages equivalent to those paid to women. Fourth, *Mutah* (gang) labour system came into existence. Fifth, wage rates also increased. Women's wage rates increased from Rs. 5 to 10, while men were paid Rs. 10 to 20.

In all the villages, the schools were started, and replaced the earlier Brahmin-teacher based education system. This, however, did not improve literacy significantly due to rash treatment by teachers, and the emergence of child labour system. People started using allopathic medicines and visit hospitals for treatment.

The Period of Post-1980

The land market became more competitive with rising land and lease values. The value of one acre of land increased to Rs. 60,000. With growing population, the land-man ratio declined. Further, with lease value going up to Rs. 4,000 per acre, and prevalence of advance payment system, it became practically impossible for resource-poor households to access land for cultivation.

The lift irrigation system became more widespread, and much of the land in these villages was receiving irrigation facilities. The cultivation of commercial crops such as paddy, cotton, tobacco, red gram and chillies got intensified. Use of fertilisers and pesticides increased.

The introduction of labour displacing technology (such as tractors, threshers and weedicides) has had adverse impact on the availability of work especially for men. Hence, they started to look for non-agricultural wage work or non-farm activities. Women and children were mainly participating in agricultural wage market.

The wages for women increased from Rs. 20 to 40, and varied on the basis of season. Men were paid Rs. 50-60 for agricultural work, and Rs. 70 for non-agricultural wage work. The poor households normally demanded that children be included in *Mutah* labour groups. So much so that in each *Mutah* labour group, about half of the labourers were children while the rest were women. This suggests the feminisation of agricultural wage labour market in these villages.

Further, although the wages had been increasing in nominal terms, the perception was that they were not increasing in real terms. One of the key informants (SC woman agricultural labourer) noted that Rs. 5 was the daily wage rate about 30 years ago when the cost of one bag of rice was Rs.100. By 1998, the wages increased to Rs. 40, but, the cost of a bag of rice increased to Rs. 1,500!

The literacy rates did not pick up despite the opportunities such as free hostels provided to SC children due to the prevalence of child labour system, and lack of employment opportunities for the educated children. The people were utilising the Primary Health Care Centres and private hospitals. The better-off went to nursing homes, and private doctors.

As far as the government support was concerned, the public distribution system had become more popular. So also, the old age pension, support to pregnant mothers and girl children, food to school going children and loans from the banks.

A Brief Note on the Selected Villages

The selected villages are located in the relatively 'backward' western part of Krishna district, and about 50 kms away from the city of Vijayawada. The selected villages are similar in the following respects: (i) though much of the cultivation in these villages is rain fed, a few farmers have well irrigation and/or draw irrigation water from the river Krishna; (ii) important crops in all these villages are tobacco, cotton, chillies, groundnut, paddy and greengram (Table 4.3); (iii) The agricultural labourers get wage work for about nine months with demand for labour reaching the peak for three months. During the slack season, they stay at home repairing their huts, attending the marriages, visiting relatives, etc., and/or migrate to eastern part of the district to work in the paddy fields. The main difference across the villages is size; while Bathinapadu is the smallest, Kothapeta is the largest village. The second difference is that Scheduled Castes (SCs) are the only community residing in Bathinapadu, while in the other village upper caste of Kamma and artisan castes reside along with the SC households.

Wealth ranking[18] exercises in the selected villages were conducted to obtain the distribution of households by wealth categories (Table 4.4). The people participating in the exercises used assets (land, housing, livestock, jewellery, etc.), employment, education, health, transportation facilities, child labour and dowry to categorise the households. Because people adopted a broader perspective on poverty to classify the households, the proportions of very poor and poor in the total households were higher ranging from about 62 per cent in Kothapet to about 78 per cent in S. Amaravaram. The proportions of very poor and poor were higher among the SC households as compared to others in Kothapeta and S. Amaravaram. The principal characteristics of the very poor were: landlessness, assetlessness, inadequate shelter (inability to repair houses), higher dependency ratio, unemployment, inability to send children to school, limited access to health facilities, etc. The poor also had almost the same characteristics. But, the ownership of a few assets and lower dependency ratio made them less vulnerable, and their dependence on moneylenders was relatively less.

Table 4.3: Some select aspects of the selected villages

Particulars	Bathinapadu	Kothapeta	S. Amaravaram
Total number of households	142	341	233
Important caste groups	Scheduled Castes (SCs)	Kammas, SCs and artisan castes	Kammas, SCs and artisan castes
Important crops	Tobacco, cotton, chillies, greengram and groundnut	Paddy, tobacco, cotton, chillies and greengram	Cotton, tobacco, chillies, groundnut and paddy
Government facilities	School, gram panchayat, Public Distribution System (PDS)	School, PDS, public Health Centre (PHC) and gram panchayat	School, PDS, PHC and gram panchayat
Non-farm employment opportunities	Petty trades such as selling of vegetables, ice and quarrying	Petty trades, services such as hotels, etc., and quarrying	Petty trades, services and quarrying.

Source: Resource mapping in the selected villages.

Table 4.4 : Distribution of households in the Andhra villages by wealth categories

Particulars	Bathinapadu		Kothapeta			S.Amaravaram		
	SCs (%)	Total in number	SCs (%)	Others (%)	Total in number	SCs (%)	Others (%)	Total in number
Very poor	100.00	49 (34.5)	86.2 (51.7)	13.8 (12.5)	123 (36.1)	51.1 (54.1)	48.9 (29.7)	90 (38.6)
Poor	100.00	47 (33.1)	50.6 (22.0)	49.4 (32.4)	89 (26.1)	26.9 (29.4)	73.1 (46.0)	93 (39.9)
Middle	100.00	19 (13.4)	21.1 (7.3)	78.9 (41.1)	71 (20.8)	35.9 (16.5)	64.1 (16.9)	39 (16.8)
Rich	100.00	27 (19.0)	67.2 (19.0)	32.8 (14.0)	58 (17.0)	0.0 (0.0)	100.0 (7.4)	11 (4.7)
All Classes	100.00	142 (100.0)	60.1 (100.0)	39.9 (100.0)	341 (100.0)	36.5 (100.0)	63.5 (100.0)	233 (100.0)

Note: Figures in parentheses are column percentages.
Source: Wealth ranking exercises conducted in the selected villages.

Severity of Poverty

The work availability was somewhat similar across the three villages. Availability of work was high during August to October, and declined in December. The landless households migrated to either eastern Krishna or to Godavari in search of work in January and stayed there for almost three months. Between May and July, the availability of work was less especially for women.

There were differences between men and women in work availability and wages. Since men participated in both agricultural and non-agricultural activities, the employment availability was more in their case. The participation of women was almost confined to agricultural labour market, and thus, feminisation of agricultural labour market was taking place. The wages for women were also less.

The incidence of diseases was relatively high during the agriculturally slack season. It was during this season that they had to borrow money not only for consumption and health expenditure but also for education as the schools were opened.

The agricultural labour households consumed three meals per day during the peak agricultural season or during the migration period. During this period, each meal consisted of rice, vegetables and meat also. However, in the month of May, they ate one or two meals and drank porridge. During the scarcity months, women ate the left over after serving the children and men. In Bathinapadu village, the participants in the seasonality mapping noted that adults in 30 to 40 per cent of the poorest households skipped meals during the slack season; a bulk of them were women.

Causes of Poverty

What are the causes of poverty? In order to find out an answer to this question, focus group interviews were held with a group of persons belonging to very poor and poor categories in five localities across the selected villages. The participants in the focus group interviews not only came up with a list of causes of poverty, but also ranked them (Table 4.5). The important causes were lack of land and unemployment in all the localities across the selected villages. Lack of land was ranked as the first cause in Kothapeta and S. Amaravaram, while it was ranked as the second in Bathinapadu and in SC locality of Kothapeta. Unemployment was ranked as the first cause for poverty in Bathinapadu, while it was ranked as the second in the other two villages. In all the localities, higher dependency ratio was mentioned as a cause of poverty though the ranking was not the same across the villages. The pattern of ranking indicates that unproductive spending on alcohol and gambling, droughts and floods, and female headed households were other important causes, while the rest did not seem to be general for all the villages. Interestingly, lack of capital to invest in agriculture and rural non-farm activities was not considered as a cause in the upper caste localities. The causes such as illiteracy and laziness were mentioned in S. Amaravaram.

Table 4.5: Ranking the causes of poverty across the selected villages

Causes	Bathinapadu	Kothapeta		S.Amaravaram	
		SCs	Others	SCs	Others
Unemployment	1	2	2	2	2
Lack of land	2	2	1	1	1
Lack of capital to invest in agriculture and petty business	3	5			
Lack of house	4				
Lack of capacity	5		4		
More number of dependants	6	3	6	4	5
Lack of social recognition (caste discrimination)	7			7	
Unanticipated crisis (accidents, etc.)	8				
Droughts and floods	9	6			9
Single women			3		4
Alcoholism and gambling		4	5	3	7
Ill-health			7		3
Illiteracy				6	6
Laziness				5	

Source: Focus group interviews conducted in the selected villages.

Conclusions

The magnitude of poverty varied within and across the villages. In general, most of the poor households belonged to the SC community. The severity of poverty also varied; in general, it was more among the SC households. Even among these households, the women bore the brunt of poverty. The principal causes of poverty were lack of endowment (lack of assets such as land), and exchange failures (unemployment). The historical analysis shows that commercialisation of agriculture mainly contributed to widespread poverty.

Notes

1. This was done with the help of two to three elders in each of the villages. The yardstick used to recall the changes was different in each case; some used important events (such as birth of a child), some others used their age (i.e., when the person was 15 years old, 25 years old, etc.), and one person used the different political rules (such as Congress rule, etc.). In these exercises, PRA techniques were used to facilitate the respondent to recall the changes, and quantify the extent of change.
2. This was true for a majority of the agricultural population in the district (Janakarajan 1996).
3. Although oil engines began to replace *kavalais* from the First World War, the growth was slow from 12 in 1915 to 150 in 1947 in the district (Bandara 1977: 326).
4. At the district level, the area under tank irrigation was higher than that under wells in 1950 (Bandara 1977: 324).
5. From 1965 onwards, the proportion of area under tanks declined, while that under wells increased in the district (Bandara 1977: 324).
6. The number of diesel engines in the district increased only to about 5,500 in 1960.
7. The area under HYVs to total area under paddy increased from 0.2 per cent in 1967-68 to 56.5 per cent in 1970-71. The area under HYVs and improved varieties to total area under paddy increased from 7.4 to 81 per cent during the same period (Chinnappa 1977: 94).
8. Chinnappa (1977: 116) reports a relatively larger proportion of the households belonging to depressed caste who adopted HYV technology in the villages close to our study villages.
9. See Harris (1993) and Harris-White and Janakarajan, (1997), for more details.
10. All the mapping exercises in the villages show that the wages in non-agricultural activities were higher than the agricultural wages. Added to that, the growth was also higher.
11. The purpose of the exercise was to classify households by wealth categories with the help of criteria evolved by the people themselves. This was done separately in the localities of upper castes, depressed castes, and so on.
12. The criteria adopted included the following: (i) basic needs (food, clothing, shelter, dependency ratio within the households and income); (ii) assets (land, cattle, savings and jewellery); (iii) well-being (ability to access and utilise the school and hospital facilities); (iv) employment [type of

employment (farm or non-farm, casual or permanent), unemployment and child labour]; (v) isolation [female headed households, help (or lack of it) from the government and community]; and (vi) dependency (borrowing, etc.).

13. This exercise was used to find out the severity of poverty in different months and whether it varied across the household members.
14. This exercise was utilised to find out the various causes of poverty, strategies adopted to overcome poverty, etc.
15. Also, see, Harris-White and Janakarajan (1997).
16. Cultural norms stipulate that Muslim women should have a veil on their faces and stay within their houses.
17. Even the poorest household has to give gifts and other alms to relatives, the needy, etc.
18. The purpose of the exercise was to rank households in terms of wealth with the help of criteria evolved by the people themselves. This was done separately in the localities of upper castes and depressed castes. The variables that were considered were the same across the localities; but, the way these were looked at varied across the localities. For instance, the people in the SC locality considered the very poor and poor as those who did not own land; but, in the same village, the people from the upper caste locality considered the people with less than one acre of land as the poor. Hence, the results have been presented across localities.

5

Poverty Alleviation Strategies of NGOs

Introduction

There is a widespread belief (and acceptance) in India that NGOs, by virtue of being small in scale, flexible, innovative, participatory, focused on development and relatively independent, are more successful in reaching the poor and in poverty alleviation. This has contributed to the increasing popularity of the NGOs among the government and external aid agencies, and their rapid growth.

The emergence of NGOs as important development actors in India implies that one can hope for more attention to the needs and concerns of the poor. This raises a number of questions. What has been the experience of NGOs in poverty alleviation and empowerment of women? Have they generated and facilitated the possibilities for the poor (especially women) to come out of poverty? Have they succeeded in enabling women to exert influence on social, economic and political processes?

The analysis on the condition and severity of poverty together with historical processes generating poverty in the last chapter suggests that relative poverty between the poor and the well-off and also within the SC households seems to have increased. Further, the nature of livelihood options differ across the villages, and also between men and women; so also, the condition and severity of poverty. Faced with this kind of situation, what activities were undertaken by the NGOs to alleviate poverty? This chapter seeks to look into this question by looking at the evidence from the two project areas.

Poverty Alleviation Interventions of SHARE

SHARE has been selected as a case study because this organisation seeks to reduce poverty by empowering its women members by initiating activities aimed at income generation and provision of non-economic benefits. Secondly, as a membership based organisation it involves members in planning, implementation and monitoring of all the development activities. This means that the organisation has to be accountable (as defined by Edwards and Hulme 1995) to its members, and has to adopt principles of good governance, transparency and simple style of functioning.

Genesis

In the late 1970s, the Christian Medical College (a well-known medical hospital located in Vellore town) found that the poor in the hinterland were unable to access medical facilities due to acute poverty while the better-off from distant places were able to. To fulfil its moral responsibility to the local population, it facilitated the formation of a few organisations in the locality to work for the economic development of the poor so that they can access the health facilities.

One of these organisations was SHARE, which was registered as a NGO in 1992. It now works with about 4,000 women belonging to landless and marginal farmer households in 40 villages. SHARE enables the poor women to undertake income generating activities through skill upgradation, marketing and raw material support. SHARE initiated income earning opportunities like palm leaf craft, sisal fibre craft, korai mat weaving, etc. In 27 villages, craft centres were started for this purpose. SHARE provides raw materials and sells the finished products in the national and international markets. In 1995-96, products worth Rs. 30.53 lakhs were sold; of which, 99 per cent were sold in the foreign market (Rajamma and Nadarajan 1997). About 600 women workers in SHARE craft centres earned a profit of Rs.1,079,962 in 1995-96 (*ibid*). An internal study revealed that incomes of members increased by 30 to 50 per cent.

But, SHARE realised the following limitations of working only in income generation: first, it was costly to provide training in palm leaf production, and supplying raw materials. Though, continuous stream of orders for palm leaf products kept coming, they were difficult to be executed as the trained women constantly dropped-out; second, older women with experience in agricultural work preferred to work as agricultural labourers rather than going through the process of obtaining training to become craft workers; third, craft activity was assigned low status by certain groups; and fourth, it was perceived that SHARE worked for the depressed castes. Poor women from the upper castes did not like to work in the production centre along with women from depressed castes. Because of the above, SHARE could not cover all the poor in the target villages. How to cover the large number of the poor in the target villages was the question.

More importantly, SHARE recognised the importance of structural aspects which constrained women to play an active role in decision-making within the community and wider arena. For instance, a key person within the organisation writes that: "Is it enough for SHARE to confine itself to activities and programmes relating to income generation and welfare? Is it not necessary for SHARE to widen its area of operation to encompass issues and matters that will be helpful in the long run to make it possible for women to increase their level of participation in decision-making at the community level? If at all this becomes necessary, what role can SHARE play in making this possible?" (Murugesan 1999: 155-56). After discussing these questions, SHARE decided to undertake the following activities for poverty reduction.

First, SHGs were formed from 1995 onwards for both craft members and other poor in the project area with the purpose of: (i) covering a large number of the poor in the project area; (ii) providing opportunities for women to undertake income generation activities as it was realised that the possibilities for all the poor to earn sufficient and secure income were limited in the craft activity; and (iii) creating a forum where women could come together to discuss their problems and take a collective action. An animator, appointed by the SHARE, took lead in the formation and strengthening of groups; subsequently, the group leaders took an active part in the management of the group.

The second activity provided awareness and training (in craft centres, SHG meetings and by SHARE in its office) on development of women, women's rights in family and society, leadership skills and personality improvement to help the women to move a step forward on the road to empowerment (Murugesan 1999).

Third, resource mobilisation from the government and banks by empowering the women. SHARE provided information on various government programmes which were meant for the poor and helped the members in accessing the resources. A significant proportion of the members possessed good knowledge about various government schemes, which were availed by some of them.

Fourth, enabling the women to contest and win gram panchayat elections. Awareness and training programmes were organised for both the animators and the women members in 1995 on decentralised government. Of the 13 women who contested for ward positions, five won, while none of the three women contesting for presidentship won in the elections (Murugesan 1999).

These activities have now been under implementation since 1996 while craft activity has been going on since 1992. Below, we discuss the impact of these activities on poverty reduction.

Impact of Craft Activity on the Poor

For analysing the impact of SHARE's development activities such as craft activity and SHGs on the incomes of the poor, vulnerability and qualitative aspects, we collected data from 84 women. We interviewed all the craft members in the selected villages, a few members of SHGs and those women who were neither involved in the craft activity nor SHG members. In all, data were collected from 44 women from Sabthalipuram; of them, 22 were craft members, 12 SHG members and 10 others. In Mottupalayam, data were collected from 40 women; of them, nine were craft members, 22 SHG members and nine others. While craft members were receiving assistance from SHARE for over eight years, the SHG members were receiving assistance for the last two years. The category of others served the purpose of control group.

Incomes of the Poor

Craft centres were started in both the villages in 1980s. In Sabthalipuram, craft activity was taken up in a rented house, while in Mottupalayam it was carried out in a community hall. In both the places, a monitor (woman) looked after the craft centre; she checked the raw material stock and ordered for more material when required, prepared dyes required for the palm leaf products, supplied raw materials to women producers, made a note of finished products by each of the women producer, and paid wages after deducting raw material charges. She had a quality controller in each of the craft centres. The payment to the monitor, based mainly on a system of incentives, was done by SHARE from the profits of craft activity. The women and school-completed (or dropped-out) girls joined the craft centre after obtaining training either by the monitor or by SHARE at Vellore.

During 1998-99, 26 women worked in the craft centre at Sabthalipuram, while the number was 11 in Mottupalayam. The number of women workers declined between 1994-95 and 1998-99 (Table 5.1) because of the composition of the group. Girls constituted a significant proportion of members. After obtaining training and working for 2-3 years, they get married and go to different villages. If they happened to go to a village where SHARE craft centre was operating, they would join in that craft centre. Otherwise, they might have to find different occupation. Between 1994-95 and 1998-99, over 50 per cent of the members stayed in Sabthalipuram craft centre: the corresponding proportion in Mottupalayam was around 30 per cent.

There were also differences in the period during which the members worked in the craft centre in a year. Although a significant proportion of members in both the years worked for the entire year, quite a few of them worked for less than nine months, and in some cases, for a period of less than three months in a year. The reasons for this were as follows: (i) a few of the members undertook agricultural labour work during the off-season and/or withdrawn to work on their own land; (ii) some of the members gave less importance to this work when they had to help their husbands in their business, or, when they had to help children in their examinations,etc.; (iii) the women withdrew from the work during child-bearing and caring periods; (iv) at times, the orders to SHARE from buyers were low and hence, there might not be work for those members who developed skills relating only to that product; and (v) in rainy season, production could not take place due to dampness which spoiled the leaves.

Table 5.1: Working months for craft members in the selected villages

Name of the village	Distribution of members by number of working months in 1994-95					Distribution of members by number of working months in 1998-99					Number of members who continuously worked in the craft centre between 1994 and 1999
	0-3	4-6	7-9	10-12	Total	0-3	4-6	7-9	10-12	Total	
Sabthalipuram	3	8	4	16	31	3	0	8	15	26	17
Mottupalayam	10	3	4	12	29	2	1	0	8	11	7

Data on 24 women producers (Table 5.2) who were working in the craft centers at both the points in time showed that the average annual income and per-month income of members from craft activity increased between 1994-95 and 1998-99 in both the places. Although the incomes of craft members in Sabthalipuram increased at a faster rate, the level of income was lower here as compared to Mottupalayam.

Table 5.2: Wages (in rupees) paid to craft members in the selected villages (1994-95 and 1998-99)

Name of the village and members	Total income		Per month income	
	1994-95	1998-99	1994-95	1998-99
MOTTUPALAYAM				
S. Vasantha	2,809	5,317	255	483
G. Poosanam	3,107	2,210	282	201
G. Vasantha	2,732	5,479	248	498
K. Valarmathi	2,738	5,787	249	526
G. Venda	2,809	8,317	255	756
G. Salammal	1,381	1,987	124	181
K. Kantha	3,516	8,495	320	772
SABTHALIPURAM				
Rahamathbi	2,190	4,570	211	415
Ashmathbi	3,147	10,048	282	913
Gulzarbi	3,599	5,225	343	475
Jagadheeshwari	2,721	6,984	251	635
Daulathbi	963	5,260	96	478
Zakirabi	2,293	8,827	288	621
R. Padma	1,190	4,521	102	411
Tharangani	1,539	2,287	153	208
Mahalakshmi	1,643	3,317	152	302
Bhanubi	2,917	7,504	253	682
V. Padmavathi	1,365	156	136	14
G. Shanthi	2,223	4,560	196	415
Amothibi	1,080	3,854	108	350
Dilsathbi	855	2,813	85	256
Myil	980	3,363	95	306
Begumbi	1,185	7,081	111	644
Zarinabi	105	3,223	11	293

One noteworthy feature of monthly incomes of members was the wide variation in both the villages at both points in time, although the variance in Sabthalipuram was higher as compared to Mottupalayam. The discussions with members of craft centres also revealed that their incomes tended to be low during certain months, and this was due to the following factors.

First, the domestic chores that women had to undertake did not leave much time to concentrate on craft activity. For instance, the monthly income for Dilsathbi in Sabthalipuram was Rs.250, while the same for others was Rs. 500-900. When asked for the reasons, she mentioned that between 5 and 11 a.m. she was involved in cooking, fetching water, cleaning, etc. For about four hours, Dilsathbi worked on craft activity, and returned home at 3 p.m. to help her husband, who worked as a quarry worker, in preparing implements for the following day. From 5 p.m. she was again involved in domestic chores. The household of Dilsathbi was large with five dependants (two elderly persons and three children) and two workers, and much of the day time was spent in taking care of the dependants. Other women in the craft centre were able to earn larger monthly incomes mainly because they had either support from family members (at times, husbands and in-laws helped them in completing the work) and/or involved girl children in domestic chores so that they could free themselves for craft work.

Second, those earning larger incomes were able to do so as they took the work to homes. Whether they could undertake the work at home or not depended on the atmosphere in the household. For instance, Kantha from Mottupalayam was able to earn the highest income in Mottupalayam craft centre because she worked up to 12 in the mid-night. Her husband did not object to this as she was the only earning member (her husband was not working due to illness). Her neighbour and relative, Vasantha, could not undertake craft activity at home after dinner because her husband did not like her working very late in the night. Hence, Vasantha worked only at the craft centre, and earned around Rs. 450 a month.

Third, some of the women members were able to earn larger incomes because more than one worker from the household were involved in the activity. As a member of the craft centre, Begambi took raw materials to home so that her deserted daughter and she could work on the craft activity. In their case, the average monthly income of Rs. 644 was to be treated as income of two persons.

Notwithstanding these factors which constrained some of the women members to earn larger income, they played an important role in providing employment and income to the craft women as compared to SHG members and others in the village. First, while all the craft members were involved in income earning activity, a large proportion of SHG members and others were not involved in any income earning activity. Second, the income from craft activity accounted for a larger proportion of total income in the case of a significant proportion of craft members (Table 5.3). The corresponding proportion was lower in the case of SHG members and others in both the villages. Third, the average income earned by the members through craft had been higher compared to that earned by the SHG members and others (Table 5.4).

Table 5.3 : Distribution of women respondents by proportion of their income to the total household income

Size class of income of the members to total income (%)	Sabthalipuram				Mottupalayam			
	Craft	SHG	Others	Total	Craft	SHG	Others	Total
0	0	10	3	13	0	1	3	4
< 20	2	6	1	9	1	8	2	11
20-40	4	3	3	10	9	0	3	12
40-80	3	1	2	6	3	1	1	5
80 >	0	2	0	2	9	2	1	12
Total	9	22	9	40	22	12	10	44

Table 5.4 also shows an inverse relationship between the average individual income of the women belonging to three categories and average household income across the size classes. This suggests the following. First, a majority of the households where women's income formed more than 80 per cent of the total household income were headed by women, or male members did not contribute income due to illness, drinking, etc. Second, the women were likely to be involved in economic activities only when men did not earn sufficient income for the household.

Table 5.4: Distribution of women respondents by their average annual income in Sabthalipuram viilage

Size classes of income to total income (per cent)	Craft members		SHG		Others	
	Average income of members (Rs.)	Average household income (Rs.)	Average income of members (Rs.)	Average household income (Rs.)	Average income of members (Rs.)	Average household income (Rs.)
0	0	0	0	12,625	0	9,300
< 20	2,200	13,800	450	8,450	1,000	5,150
20 - 40	6,567	19,600	0	0	3,967	11,700
40 - 80	4,267	13,733	2,000	2,000	4,000	9,000
80 >	5,733	7,847	2,700	4,100	3,000	3,000
Total	5,714	13,728	654	10,220	2,090	8,530

Thus, notwithstanding variations in the incomes of members due to differences in skills, involvement in domestic work and support within the household, the incomes had increased in recent years. Has the vulnerability of women and households come down?

Vulnerability

Vulnerability means susceptibility to contingencies such as physical incapacity, disasters, social needs, unproductive expenditure, seasonal adversity and lack of food, and exploitation (Chambers 1988: 14). SHARE formed SHGs for the poor women to enable them to save and thereby, reducing vulnerability.

A community organiser from SHARE formed SHGs and provided awareness relating to leadership development, group cohesion, savings, internal revolving of savings for credit, building linkages with government agencies, etc. In both the villages, the members saved Rs. 30 to Rs. 50 per month. The savings in the case of craft members were regular as they had craft income while they were irregular in the case of SHG members. The savings mobilised in a group were lent to members for consumption and working capital at 24 per cent interest rate. A loan was to be returned in 5 to 12 monthly instalments depending on the loan amount. The decisions were taken by the members themselves.

Table 5.5 shows that there were three SHGs in Mottupalayam and two in Sabthalipuram. Based on months and year of formation, the levels of savings varied. However, SHGs for craft members (Sampangi in Mottupalayam and Parijatham in Sabthalipuram) were started in 1996, and hence, the level of savings in these groups was much higher. The savings, the members note, gave some security to face disasters and meet the social needs.

Secondly, the savings were also revolved (Table 5.6). In two and half years between July 1996 and February 1999, 11 out of 18 members in Parijatham group took a loan amount of Rs. 29,700. Eight out of 18 members had taken two or more loans for consumption and production activities. The ratio of savings to loan amount was 1:3 and this implied a faster revolving of savings amount. Similarly, seven out of ten members in Sampangi group took two or more loans for consumption and production. The ratio of savings to credit was 1:2

Table 5.5: Details of savings mobilised by SHGs in the selected villages

Name of the village and group	Month and year of formation	Total Number of members	Distribution of members by savings amount in Rs.					Total savings in Rs.
			< 200	201 - 500	501 - 1000	>1000	Total	
MOTTUPALAYAM								
Sampangi	September 1996	10	0	0	0	10	10	15,160
Deepam Bharatha	September 1998	10	9	1	0	0	10	1,720
Matha	November 1998	11	8	3	0	0	11	1,510
SABTHALIPURAM								
Parijatham	July 1996	18	3	0	15	0	18	9,300
Sivan	April 1997	14	0	14	0	0	14	5,620
Total		63						33,310

in this group. The functioning of SHGs among craft members suggested that they had provided credit facilities to large proportion of members to meet expenditures relating to food, education, health, social needs, etc. The loans had also been utilised to face the disasters. For instance, Kantha's husband became suddenly ill and had to undergo a surgical operation. Her craft earnings were used to meet the consumption needs. Hence, a loan was required to meet the expenditure on the operation. The SHG came to her rescue.

Table 5.6: Details of credit operations in the selected villages

Name of the village and groups	Total amount of loan given (Rs.)	Distribution of members by number of loans				
		0	1	2	3	4
MOTTUPALAYAM						
Sampangi	33,800	3	0	2	4	1
Deepam	5,000	6	4	0	0	0
Bharatha Matha	2,000	10	1	0	0	0
SABTHALIPURAM						
Parijatham	29,700	7	3	5	2	1
Sivan	9,500	7	4	2	1	0

Has the credit facility enabled the women to start income generation activities? The information on livelihood options available to women respondents shows that occupational diversification had taken place in the case of most of the craft members. In the case of a significant proportion of craft members, the household members were involved in craft activity, wage labour in agriculture and non-agricultural occupations such as quarrying, construction, beedi-rolling, etc. The occupational diversification was not all that evident in the case of SHG members. This was because of the following reasons: first, the credit from SHGs had been mainly availed for consumption purposes such as health, education, etc.; and second, in some cases, credit had been availed for agriculture; but, that had not resulted in occupational diversification.

Another major reason for the insignificant occupational diversification was limited opportunities, and constraints to diversify their income earning opportunities. For instance, a Muslim woman was a member of the SHG for over 2 years. Although she was eligible to take loan from the group, she had not availed the opportunity because of the following reasons: (i) she could not undertake livestock rearing activity as the household did not own a house, and hence, a place to keep livestock was not available; (ii) she could not open a petty shop because she did not have any male support. Her husband was alcoholic and she could not trust him to bring provisions from Vellore town, or to run the business; and (iii) she herself could not run the business because of social factors. The societal sanctions came in the way of her going to market on her own or to sit in the petty shop. A majority of the women in craft centre and SHGs noted that they did not have skills to undertake income generating activity. Further, the income generating opportunities seemed to be low in these villages as the non-agricultural labour market was segmented along caste and gender lines.

Hence, notwithstanding increased incomes from craft activity and savings and credit facility from SHGs, the women still felt vulnerable. For instance, Padma and her son are now leading a comfortable life. With a monthly income of Rs. 1,500 from her craft and son's quarry work, the household does not have livelihood problems. In fact, they have been saving large amounts every month to construct a house. When asked about vulnerability, both mother and son felt that if something happened to one of them, the household will be in a crisis. The accidents in quarry work are common, and some of the workers in the village have become physically disabled due to quarry-related accidents. The fear of disaster occurring is so high that they are reluctant to borrow for house construction, and hence, are saving money to construct a house.

Dilsathbi also noted that her household faced vulnerability. With five dependants, the household mainly depended on the earnings of her husband from quarry activity. Recently, her husband fell ill and could not work for a fortnight. The entire household was facing uncertainty owing to illness of the principal earning member.

In contrast, Vasantha, a craft member, did not feel vulnerable. Although her earnings from craft activity were meagre, her husband earned sufficient income from the business of selling aluminium vessels. They also had land from which they got annual supplies of paddy. The case of Vasantha suggests that the possession of productive assets was important in whether a household faced vulnerability or not. Most of the craft members were landless, and hence, they faced vulnerability notwithstanding a rise in money incomes in most of the cases.

Qualitative Improvements

Since SHARE has been working with craft members for the last 8 years, the evidence presented mainly relates to them. After becoming members in the craft centre, women stated that they now had an opportunity to discuss about their personal problems, and were provided with awareness on several issues. The craft women noted that their skills in craft activity improved, and this built confidence in them. They also noted that the personal problems were discussed in the craft centre; counselling was provided to women in distress.

Control Over Incomes

The incomes from craft activity, though meagre, are valued by members. Ragejabi and her daughter together earned Rs. 644 from the craft activity. When she was asked to rank the local organisations, craft centre and Public Distribution System (PDS) were given high importance. According to her, "because there is PDS, we are able to purchase foodgrains although we have low income from the craft centre. At the same time, without craft income, we would not have been in a position to purchase foodgrains from PDS". Another woman earned Rs. 600 per month and this constituted only a small proportion of total income of the household (with her husband's business income forming the bulk). She utilised this income for household expenditure, and also to give gifts to her own relatives. She stated that she valued this small income as this enabled her to have personal freedom with regard to expenditure.

Begumbi is 45 years old and earns around Rs. 600 per month. She was not at all working after her marriage. Her husband was earning income from quarrying. Her son ran away from home, and this had an adverse impact on her husband. He started drinking, and soon suffered from paralytic stroke. He could not work and earn any income. With four dependants at home, Begumbi had to earn income. She joined in the craft activity after obtaining training. Her husband, who did not allow her to work after the marriage, not only now allowed her to work, but also stopped doing any work. In addition, he borrowed for his drinking, and expected Begumbi to repay the loans. With higher dependency ratio and drinking of her husband, the income of Rs. 600 per month was only sufficient to buy essential foodgrains, but insufficient for buying milk, vegetables and meat products. Although she made decisions on the utilisation of income, and asserted her views regarding day-to-day running of the households, she felt disempowered because the society expected her husband to make decisions with regard to crucial issues such as marriage, etc. Her husband stole money from her belongings, and put pressure on her to borrow from the SHG for his drinking. Though she did not succumb to his pressures, she felt quite burdened.

The experience of Kantha can be considered as a successful case as far as control over income is concerned. Kantha's husband was an ambitious person; he started aluminium selling business as well as leasing in land with outside borrowing at exorbitant interest rates. Soon, there were losses, and the debts got accumulated. All his business ventures came to a standstill and Kantha had to earn from the craft centre to take care of the household. In addition, her husband became ill and had to be operated. As noted earlier, Kantha borrowed money for the operation and also repaid. Added to that, the creditors started pressing for repayment, and some of them also used abusive language. Pained by these developments, Kantha not only started working hard but also began repaying debts. Her husband, now recovered, has begun to assert as far as the utilisation of income was concerned. Kantha shouted back at her husband by saying that "your poor judgement landed us in trouble. I have repaid all the loans taken by you. I have proved that I have better judgement in financial matters than you. Hence, do not again interfere". She states that her husband does not now assert his role in the utilisation of her income as he was doing earlier.

Thus, the evidence on control over incomes is mixed. Quantitative data also corroborates this. Of the total craft and SHG members who are earning income, a majority have passed on their earnings to either husbands or father. Of those members who retain income, a majority spends their earning for household purposes. Very small proportion of women retains their earnings for personal needs. Thus, those women, who earn income, do not convert income to meet their personal needs or to improve their welfare.

A large proportion of craft and SHG members stated that either decisions were made by self and husband, or by husband alone. The pattern did not vary much between craft members and others.

Has the craft activity or membership in SHG improved mobility for women? Given that many women did not undertake income generating activities, their mobility seemed to be limited either to craft centre or to their workplace in agriculture or non-agriculture. We asked the women regarding their mobility outside the house such as going to the town on their own. A large proportion of women belonging to three categories stated that they went out only with their husbands or with parents. Even if some women went out, they had to seek permission to do so.

However, there is some awareness relating to government programmes and local decentralised government. All the craft members as well as a majority of the SHG members possess knowledge of various government programmes (such as widow pension, old age pension, incentives to girl education, etc.). A majority of them have also accessed these benefits mainly through the staff member of SHARE. They stated that collective strategies were not very effective in mobilising the government resources.

Similarly, craft members are aware of the reservations provided to women to contest in the local panchayats. They are also aware of mandatory gram sabha meetings. But, the widespread opinion among them is that gram panchayat does not have much role to play in poverty alleviation.

Conclusions

As a membership based organisation, SHARE has been responsive and responsible in assessing the changing needs of members, and formulating and implementing programmes in response to these changing needs.

The craft activity started by the organisation is successful in so far as enabling women members to obtain employment and earning incomes. Although incomes tend to be small and uncertain, they are valued by women members. Skills relating to craft activity were acquired and thereby, improving the confidence in members. Craft centre provides the women an opportunity to come together every-day and discuss their personal problems. In the process, awareness and knowledge on government programmes and gram panchayats were acquired.

SHGs were started to cover a larger proportion of the poor and to provide a forum for women to come together. Since they were formed only two years ago, it is too early to assess their role in poverty alleviation and empowerment. But, the indications are that there is cohesiveness within the groups, leadership is emerging and groups are being managed by members themselves. Savings are contributed regularly, and this amount provides confidence and security to women. As of now, women mainly borrow for consumption and crop production. Not much credit is provided to initiate income generation activities. Further, not many women are coming forward to borrow for income generation as they face constraints (lack of skills and capital, inability to find an activity that can fetch them income higher than that available in wage labour, segmented non-farm labour market, societal constraints, etc.).

Another conclusion based on the evidence on proportion of women's income to total income is that women's income forms a large proportion of the total income. A majority of such households are headed by women and the contribution of male income is low (often due to illness, drinking). The evidence also suggests that enabling women to earn income may result in a situation of male members withdrawing from the labour market. As the cases of Begumbi and Kantha suggest, this phenomenon puts a lot of pressure on them. We are not suggesting that women should not be provided with opportunities to earn income; what we are suggesting is that men should also be brought within the purview of development intervention if women are to be empowered.

Although SHARE has initiated development activities with all the sincerity to empower women through income generation activities, we do not find much evidence to suggest that non-economic benefits are taking place. This indicates that economic programmes need not necessarily be a good strategy for women's empowerment. There are larger societal and political forces that constrain women to achieve empowerment especially in non-economic fields. We suggest that different types of interventions (not entirely based on economic programmes) are to be initiated, if poverty reduction is to take place.

Poverty Alleviation Interventions by Sanghamitra

Sanghamitra has been working in the western part of Krishna district since 1985 in the area of poverty alleviation and empowerment of women. In 1999, it was working in 14 villages of Kanchikacherla mandal in Krishna district. The organisation had formed 138 SHGs by 1999. The total number of members in 138 SHGs was 1,863 in 1999. On the whole, the organisation worked with 3,010 members; of them, 95 per cent were women, while the rest were men. Of them, about 50 per cent belonged to SC community *(dalits)*, the rest to minority and economically backward communities.

The main activities of the organisation are:

- self-help promotion through the formation, strengthening and consolidation of SHGs;
- building the capacity of target group members by conducting various need based training programmes; and
- formation and strengthening of the federation of SHGs, and also working with other NGOs.

The organisation began its work with child sponsorship project of Action Aid; subsequently, work relating to income generation programmes with the support from GPC/EZE and construction of houses for the poor with support from BFW were undertaken. In 1995, Sanghamitra sought funds for its 'Antyodaya' programme from GTZ/SHF for the formation of SHGs, building the capacity of members, and facilitating the formation of a federation of SHGs. Thus, there has been a shift in the development focus from child development to self-help promotion.

There has also been a shift in the focus of the target group. Sanghamitra was earlier working with men and women, but, it subsequently concentrated more on women. The target group of the organisation was defined as socially and economically backward castes, classes, in general, and specifically, SCs, STs, minorities, BCs and single women.

People's Organisations

The earliest forum used to organise women at the village level was Mahila Mandal, an umbrella organisation for all the activities. Each Mahila Mandal had an Executive Committee consisting of seven members (including President, Secretary, Treasurer, etc.). The role of the Mahila Mandal was to take up issues relating to the village as a whole. The women were also participating in small savings activity. The Mahila Mandals existed until 1995.

When the organisation came into contact with GTZ, it became interested in self-help promotion. The need to have small groups for effective savings and credit programme, and to enable group members to undertake self-help promotion activities was also realised. The organisation, therefore, wanted to bifurcate larger Mahila Mandals into smaller SHGs. Further, the larger Mahila Mandals were considered to be inappropriate to involve all the women in savings and credit activities. A bifurcation was also needed to develop linkages between SHGs and the government (DWCRA programme)/banks. It may be noted that the linkage was possible only when the groups were small with about 15 members. From 1997 onwards, the earlier Mahila Mandals were divided into SHGs. In all the villages, the methodology of group formation was based on self-selection process wherein the selection of members in each group was left to the members themselves.

As per the rules formulated by SHGs and the organisation, the monthly amount of savings contributed by each member should be Rs. 30 in the project area of Sanghamitra. However, the amount varied from Rs. 20 to Rs. 50. A savings account was opened in the bank in the name of each SHG and operated by the leaders of SHGs. The savings were to be contributed before the 10th of every month; if somebody failed to pay, they attracted a fine of Rs. 5 per day.

Savings deposited in the bank earned an interest of 5 per cent, which was passed on to the members. But, a majority of the groups also revolved savings for various activities and the interest earned was equally distributed among the members and/or added to the savings amount of members. There were also special savings in the form of recurring and fixed deposits in the banks facilitated by the organisation.

The SHG members have had access to two sources of revolving credit fund; their own savings fund and revolving credit fund operated by Sanghamitra. The revolving fund by the Sanghamitra was used for the purchase of sheep and fattening of the same, dairying, purchase of house sites, construction of houses, toilets, etc. The loans from banks in the form of DWCRA loans and from DRDA were again used for income generation. The savings of members were revolved for emergency needs, cultivation, leasing in land, common economic programme (bulk purchase of essential goods and distributing at the wholesale rate).

In order to borrow from the savings fund at SHG level, a member had to apply (in oral or written form) to the president and secretary of the group. The representatives of the group then conducted a meeting to take a decision on whether a loan was to be given or not. In the case of loans from the organisation, loan applications had to be in written form. In the case of loans from the savings fund, the decision was taken by the group itself. On the other hand, the decision-making with regard to loans from the NGOs rested with the organisation.

An important criterion to obtain a loan from the group and NGO was that a member should not have been a defaulter. The repayment amount and schedule was decided by the group. The rate of interest charged by the group on the loans to members was 24 per cent. The minimum and maximum amount of loans varied from Rs. 500 to Rs. 5,000. According to the organisation, the group members ensured that the proposed activity was feasible and viable by raising questions relating to marketing, raw-material, possible profit and economics, training needs, investment details, source of own contribution, possible sources from the government, knowledge, skill and experience, involvement of other members in the family and details of veterinary services in the case of livestock.

The principle of savings linked to credit was followed, and it varied from 1:1 in the case of consumption loans to 1:5 in the case of income generation loans. The interest rate was 12 per cent on loans given by Sanghamitra, while it was 24 per cent in the case of loans taken out of their savings.

Economic Benefits in the Project Area of Sanghamitra

From the project area of Sanghamitra, information was collected from six groups in Bathinapadu, Kothapet and S. Amaravaram villages located in Kanchikacherla mandal of Krishna district. The primary data were collected from 53 member households in four older SHGs in Kothapeta and Bathinapadu villages, and 23 households having membership in two new groups in Seri Amaravaram village. The old groups are referred to as member groups and the new groups as comparison groups.

All the members in both member and non-member groups were SCs. Most of them were landless. The landlessness was significantly less among the member group. One did not, however, find much difference between member and non-member groups in so far as marital status and education were concerned. However, the members in the comparison group appeared to be younger as compared to the member group.

Access to Credit

Between 1994 and 1999, 53 households in the member group obtained 406 loans from the group and NGO (Table 5.7). This implies that, on an average, each member had taken four loans. An interesting aspect is that the member households had taken loans for a number of activities. These were for both income generation and consumption. About 35 per cent of the loans had been taken for agriculture, and rearing of milch animals. The other purposes for which significant proportion of loans taken were for construction of toilets, site purchase and registration and acquiring gas connections.

Table 5.7: Details on loans taken by the SHG members in Sanghamitra

Purpose	Number of Loans						
	1994	1995	1996	1997	1998	1999	Total
1	2	3	4	5	6	7	8
Milch animals	100.0	0.0	0.0	22.7	1.4	1.5	9.4
Agriculture	0.0	15.3	15.1	22.7	50.0	35.8	25.4
Site Purchase/Registration	0.0	34.7	0.0	3.0	1.4	37.3	13.1
Purchase of sheep	0.0	18.1	0.0	4.5	14.9	0.0	6.7
Children's education	0.0	8.3	4.7	4.5	1.4	1.5	3.9
Current/gas	0.0	20.8	13.2	0.0	0.0	13.4	9.4
Consumption	0.0	2.8	0.0	4.5	21.6	4.5	5.9
Health purpose	0.0	0.0	1.9	9.1	6.8	3.0	3.7
Toilet doors	0.0	0.0	52.8	0.0	0.0	1.5	14.0
Marriage/functions	0.0	0.0	10.4	28.8	2.7	0.0	7.9
Others	0.0	0.0	1.9	0.0	0.0	1.5	0.7
Total (Nos.)	21	72	106	65	74	67	406
Total Loan Amount (Rs.)							
Milch animals	100.0	0.0	0.0	53.9	3.8	0.7	28.7
Agriculture	0.0	11.8	20.7	20.5	55.8	58.1	27.9

Table 5.7 *(Contd.)*

1	2	3	4	5	6	7	8
Site purchase/Registration	0.0	56.2	0.0	0.6	3.8	19.0	11.6
Purchase of sheep	0.0	16.9	0.0	3.1	10.1	0.0	5.4
Children's education	0.0	.1.1	5.1	3.6	3.1	4.4	2.8
Current/gas	0.0	11.7	11.4	0.0	0.0	7.7	4.3
Consumption	0.0	2.4	0.0	1.0	5.7	2.2	2.0
Health purpose	0.0	0.0	3.8	5.5	12.4	1.7	4.6
Toilet doors	0.0	0.0	42.3	0.0	0.0	4.8	6.7
Marriage/functions	0.0	0.0	15.7	9.8	5.3	0.0	5.6
Others (repayment of old loan, house construction, petty shop)	0.0	0.0	0.9	0.0	0.0	1.5	0.3
Total (Rs.)	94,500	92,501	88,313	134,142	130,596	68,900	608,952
Average Loan Amount (Rs.)							
Milch animals	4,500	0	0	5,000	5,000	500	4,605
Agriculture	0	991	1,144	1,833	1,970	1,667	1,647
Site purchase/registration	0	2,080	0	400	5,000	522	1,337
Purchase of sheep	0	1,200	0	1,400	1,200	0	1,222
Children's education	0	167	900	1,600	4,000	3,000	1,081
Current/gas	0	720	719	0	0	589	689
Consumption	0	1,100	0	433	464	517	520
Health purpose	0	0	1,700	1,233	3,240	600	1,880
Toilet doors	0	0	668	0	0	3,277	714
Marriage/functions	0	0	1,259	692	3,430	0	1,058
Others	0	0	400	0	0	1,000	600
Average (Rs.)	4,500	1,285	833	2,032	1,765	1,028	1,500

Purchase of Productive Assets

With access to credit from SHGs, did members improve their asset base? Table 5.8 shows that households in both member and comparison groups had not purchased land after they had become SHG members. However, a significant proportion of households from the member group acquired milch animals after they had become SHG members. In the case of other assets, the difference is not very significant.

Are households in the member group better off in terms of sources of income? The distribution of households by number of occupations in which household members were involved shows that nearly one-third of the households from the comparison group were involved only in one occupation. This happened to be agricultural labour in most of the cases. The rest obtained livelihood from two sources. In contrast, only one-fifth of the households in the member group depended on one occupation. Interestingly, about one-third of

Table 5.8: Distribution of households (%) by ownership of productive assets

(In percentages)

Assets	Members				Comparison group			
	Acquired before	Acquired after	Not acquired	Total (no.)	Acquired before	Acquired after	Not acquired	Total (no.)
Land	24.53	0.00	75.47	53	11.11	0.00	88.89	27
Milch animals	5.66	28.30	66.04	53	7.41	0.00	92.59	27
Sheep/goat	0.00	1.89	98.11	53	0.00	0.00	100.00	27
Poultry	0.00	0.00	100.00	53	3.70	3.70	92.59	27
Animals	0.00	0.00	100.00	53	0.00	0.00	100.00	27
Equipment	1.89	1.89	96.23	53	0.00	0.00	100.00	27

the households in this group obtained livelihood from 3-4 sources. This suggests that occupational diversification was more pronounced among member group households (Table 5.9).

Table 5.9: Distribution (%) of households by number of occupations

No. of occupations	Member group	Comparison group
One	21	63
Two	43	33
Three	26	4
Four	10	0
All	100	100

With occupational diversification, household income also seemed to be higher among households belonging to the member group. Table 5.10 shows that the proportion of households obtaining less than Rs. 20,000 was much higher in the comparison group. In contrast, about two-thirds of the households from the member group were obtaining more than Rs. 20,000 of annual income in 2000.

Table 5.10: Distribution (%) of households by size class of income

Size Class of income (Rs.)	Member Group	Comparison Group
<10,000	13.2	7.4
10,000 - 20,000	20.8	51.9
20,000 - 30,000	28.3	22.2
30,000 - 40,000	18.9	14.8
40,000 - 50,000	9.4	0.0
50,000 +	9.4	3.7
TOTAL (No.)	53	27

The higher average household income seems to have had a positive impact on the households acquiring consumer durables, and incurring expenditure on food, housing etc. Table 5.11 shows that none of the households in the comparison group acquired a radio, TV, scooter, wall clock. Iron box, gas stove or jewellery. On the other hand, all the households purchased gas stoves through 'Deepam' scheme introduced by the government for SHG members. While one-third of the households in the member group acquired TV, about 10 per cent acquired radio and scooter.

Table 5.11: Distribution (%) of households by consumption assets

Assets	Member Group				Comparison Group			
	Acquired before	Acquired after	Not acquired	Total (no.)	Acquired before	Acquired after	Not acquired	Total (no.)
Radio	24.5	13.2	62.3	53	7.4	0.0	92.6	27
T.V	0.0	32.1	67.9	53	7.4	0.0	92.6	27
Scooter	3.8	9.4	86.8	53	0.00	0.0	100.0	27
Wall clock	1.9	50.9	47.2	53	40.7	0.0	59.3	27
Iron box	0.0	5.7	94.3	53	0.00	0.0	100.0	27
Gas stove	0.0	100.0	0.0	53	0.00	0.0	100.0	27
Jewellery	41.5	5.7	52.8	53	44.4	0.0	55.6	27

Interestingly, over 90 per cent of the households in the member group perceived that the expenditure on food, housing, clothing, child care and health care increased after they became SHG members. A relatively larger proportion of households in the member group had also noted that the expenditure on the entertainment, social functions and education went up (Table 5.12).

Table 5.12 : Households stating that their expenditure had increased after joining SHG

(In percentages)

	Food	Housing	Clothing	Child care	Health care	Entertainment	Social functions	Travel	Education
Members	96.2	96.2	90.6	90.6	94.3	35.9	34.0	71.7	41.5
Comparison group	3.7	0.0	0.0	0.0	3.7	0.0	0.0	3.7	0.0

Social Benefits to Member Households in the Project Area of Sanghamitra

Do micro-finance programmes have positive impact on the decision-making capacity of women? If yes, does it reflect in concrete development outcomes such as educational levels between members and others? What do group members think about girl education, age at which girls should marry, participation in political institutions, etc.? These questions have been taken up for analysis in the case of the households in the project area of Sanghamitra.

Decision-Making within the Household

As in the case of the other project area, control over income has been taken as a proxy of improved decision-making. Here, two types of decisions are taken into account. First type refers to large purchases made in the last one year for the household, for children and for herself. Second type refers to important decisions relating to productive activities, education and reproductive activities made in the last five years.

Control over Income

When asked whether women were able to independently decide on the purchase of kitchen utensils, clothes for children and sarees for self, the responses varied across each of these activities and also between the groups. Between 66 and 75 per cent of the women in the member group stated that they took independent decisions with regard to the above as against 22 to 56 per cent of women in the comparison group (Table 5.13). Thus, the proportions of women independently deciding on these purchases were relatively higher in the member group as compared to the comparison group. This indicates that since women from the member group had accessed loans for the purchase of milch animals and other income generating activities, their control over income seemed to have improved.

Table 5.13 : Distribution of households (%) by large purchase made in one year (Sanghamitra)

Type of purchase	Members			Comparison group		
	Yes	No	Total (no.)	Yes	No	Total (no.)
Kitchen utensils	66.04	33.96	53	44.44	55.56	27
Clothes for children	68.67	31.33	83	22.22	77.78	27
Sarees	75.47	24.53	53	55.56	44.44	27
Family's daily food	60.38	39.62	53	51.85	48.15	27

Involvement in Major Decisions

The literature on micro-finance suggests that with gradual economic improvement and years of association with micro-finance groups resulting in empowerment process, women will be in a position to take decisions on major events in one's own life. These events could be house repair/renovation, purchase of productive assets such as milch animals and other livestock, leasing in/out of land, buying land, family planning, education of girls and boys. The primary data on decision-making on each of the above events and activities have been presented in Table 5.14. The data reveal that none of the women from the comparison group took independent decisions on the above except a few in the case of girl education. In the case of women belonging to the comparison group, most of the households were not even involved in the decisions relating to house repair/renovation, purchase of milch animals and livestock, buying of land, leasing in/out of land, and education of boys and girls in the last five years. This first of all corroborates the earlier finding that the involvement

Table 5.14 : Distribution of members (%) by their involvement in major decisions and by type of groups in the last five years

Type of decision	Members					Comparison Group			
	Own	Husband	Family members	Decision not taken	Total (no.)	Own	Husband	Decision not taken	Total (no.)
House repair/Renovation	1.89	15.09	1.89	81.13	53	0.00	11.11	88.89	27
Milch animals/Goat for profits	1.89	30.19	3.77	64.15	53	0.00	7.41	92.59	27
Leased in and leased out land	0.00	26.42	1.89	71.70	53	0.00	3.70	96.30	27
Buying of land and other assets	1.89	3.77	0.00	94.34	53	0.00	0.00	100.00	27
Family planning	7.55	52.83	0.00	39.62	53	0.00	77.78	22.22	27
Girl's education	0.00	15.09	0.00	84.91	53	3.70	7.41	88.89	27
Boy's education	0.00	18.87	0.00	81.13	53	0.00	11.11	88.89	27

of households belonging to the comparison group in the purchase of productive assets and participation of income generating activities was not as active as it was in the case of households from the member group. Whenever the households in the comparison group were involved in these decisions, it was the husband who took the decision. The pattern was different in the case of women from the member group, albeit marginally. The proportion of households involving in these decisions was relatively large in most of the cases except in the case of land purchase. In the last five years, over 60 per cent of the households in this group took decisions relating to family planning and about 40 per cent in the purchase of milch animals and other livestock. Some of the women members from this group stated that they had taken independent decision in the case of family planning, purchase of milch animals, buying of land and house repair. None of the women from this group took independent decision with regard to leasing in land and education of boys and girls.

This suggests that while women took independent decisions with regard to large purchases for the household, the same was not the case with regard to major decisions in the household. It would be, therefore, interesting to see whether this lack of autonomy had any impact on development outcomes. We took education as a proxy of development outcomes.

Literacy Rates between the Groups

Of the 244 household members belonging to the member group, nearly 46 per cent were literate. On the other hand, the literacy rate among households in the comparison group was nearly 54 per cent. Thus, literacy rates were higher in the case of household members belonging to the comparison groups in the project area of Sanghamitra. This held true for both males and females in this group. However, there was a qualitative difference in so far as high school and higher education was concerned. A larger proportion of household members from the member group had high school and college education. Some of the household members in the member group even had technical and post-graduate education. The corresponding proportions were less in the case of those from the comparison group (Table 5.15). As noted earlier, it might not be methodologically sound to look at literacy rates because these were unlikely to be influenced by the SHG membership especially when the membership period was not very long, and in the event of women joining in the group after certain age group. It is, therefore, important to look at school attendance by age groups between member and comparison groups.

Table 5.15 : Distribution (%) of all the household members by education and by sex in the project area of Sanghamitra

Education Level	Members			Comparison group		
	Male	Female	Total	Male	Female	Total
Illiterate	31.82	62.50	45.90	46.48	63.64	53.97
LKG/UKG/Primary	24.24	11.61	18.44	8.45	16.36	11.90
Middle school	17.42	11.61	14.75	18.31	5.45	12.70
High school	9.85	3.57	6.97	11.27	3.64	7.94
College	3.03	2.68	2.87	1.41	0.00	0.79
Degree	0.00	0.89	0.41	2.82	0.00	1.59
TCH Training/Technical	4.55	0.00	2.46	0.00	0.00	0.00
University	0.76	0.00	0.41	0.00	0.00	0.00
Children	8.33	7.14	7.79	11.27	10.91	11.11
Total (no.)	132	112	244	71	55	126

A distribution of all the household members by levels of education and age group for both member and comparison groups has been provided in Table 5.16. It is observed that a larger proportion of illiterates could be found in the age group of above 25 years in both member and comparison groups. Second, the proportion of illiterate household members was relatively high in the age groups of 6-14 and 15-25 years in the case of comparison group. Third, as noted earlier, the proportion of household members going to school or completing some school or college education seemed to be higher in the case of member groups. However, one could not observe the differences between member and comparison groups more strikingly.

For this reason, we constructed the proportion of members in school/literate in each of the age groups (Table 5.17). The Table, which gives the proportion of household members in school, completing education and literates in an age group to total household members in that age group, shows interesting patterns. First, the proportion of household members in school/literate to total household

Table 5.16 : Distribution of household members by education and age groups in the project area of Sanghamitra

Education Level	Members					Comparison Group				
	< 5	6 - 14	15 - 25	25 >	Total	< 5	6 - 14	15 - 25	25 >	Total
Illiterate	0	9	23	80	112	0	12	24	32	68
	(0.00)	(8.04)	(20.54)	(71.43)	(100.00)	(0.00)	(17.65)	(35.29)	(47.06)	(100.00)
LKG/UKG/ Primary	0	28	4	13	45	0	11	2	2	15
	(0.00)	(62.22)	(8.89)	(28.89)	(100.00)	(0.00)	(73.33)	(13.33)	(13.33)	(100.00)
Middle school	0	11	20	5	36	0	3	7	6	16
	(0.00)	(30.56)	(55.56)	(13.89)	(100.00)	(0.00)	(18.75)	(43.75)	(37.50)	(100.00)
High school	0	1	13	3	17	0	1	4	5	10
	(0.00)	(5.88)	(76.47)	(17.65)	(100.00)	(0.00)	(10.00)	(40.00)	(50.00)	(100.00)
College	0	0	6	1	7	0	0	0	1	1
	(0.00)	(0.00)	(85.71)	(14.29)	(100.00)	(0.00)	(0.00)	(0.00)	(100.00)	(100.00)
Degree	0	0	1	0	1	0	0	2	0	2
	(0.00)	(0.00)	(100.00)	(0.00)	(100.00)	(0.00)	(0.00)	(100.00)	(0.00)	(100.00)
TCH Training/ Technical	0	0	6	0	6	0	0	0	0	0
	(0.00)	(0.00)	(100.00)	(0.00)	(100.00)	(0.00)	(0.00)	(0.00)	(0.00)	(0.00)
University	0	0	1	0	1	0	0	0	0	0
	(0.00)	(0.00)	(100.00)	(0.00)	(100.00)	(0.00)	(0.00)	(0.00)	(0.00)	(0.00)
Children	18	1	0	0	19	14	0	0	0	14
	(94.74)	(5.26)	(0.00)	(0.00)	(100.00)	(100.00)	(0.00)	(0.00)	(0.00)	(100.00)
Total	18	50	74	102	244	14	27	39	46	126
	(7.38)	(20.49)	(30.33)	(41.80)	(100.00)	(11.11)	(21.43)	(30.95)	(36.51)	(100.00)

Note: Figures in parentheses represent percentages.

members was 47 per cent in the case of member group as against 35 per cent in the case of comparison group. Second, there was inverse relationship between age groups and the proportion of household members in school/literates. This implies that the households in both the groups were giving importance to education. The fact that the proportions for the age group of 6-14 and 15-25 were higher for the member group suggests that the households in this group gave relatively more importance to education.

Table 5.17 : Household members (%) in school or literates in the project area of Grama Vikas

Age group	Member group	Comparison group
< 5	0	0
6 - 14	82	56
15 - 25	69	38
25 and above	22	30
All age groups	47	35

This discussion shows that although women members were not directly involved in decision-making relating to education of boys and girls, the education status seemed to be qualitatively different in the case of member group. This suggests that there were other forces which were at work in improving the knowledge levels among the household members of the member group. In the case of Sanghamitra, an important reason was awareness and education imparted in group meetings. This was demonstrated by the case of Augustine (Box 5.1). Further, support to education was provided by the group through giving loans towards school fees, uniforms, etc.

Perceptions on Importance of Education and Marriage Age

The parental expectations on the purpose of education played an important role in children's education. There is, therefore, a need to examine the evidence on aspects relating to the value attached to sending children to school and whether there were any differences in the perception of members on sending children to school. When asked a question on reasons why children were sent to school, a majority of women from both the groups felt that school education would help in obtaining employment (Table 5.18). Only a few of them stated that school education brought in awareness and literacy. However, the proportion of women stating that children should be sent to school for education and awareness was high in the member group as compared to their counterparts in the project area of Sanghamitra as well as those in the comparison group. The discussions with member households revealed that many of them were aware that obtaining employment was a difficult proposition, and this came in the way of sending children (especially boys) to the school.

Box 5.1 : Augustine's fight to educate her daughter

Augustine, aged around 45 years, is an illiterate member of the oldest SHG in Bathinapadu village. She could not get education because of poverty of her parents, and was married at an early age. She learnt how to put her signature in the group. She stated that the importance of education became very evident after joining the group. As she was holding a leadership position in the group, she was required to travel to government offices to obtain resources for the group. She could not read the destination of buses, felt very handicapped in her interactions with officials (who would often say what do you illiterate know of government rules and regulations) and in undertaking leadership responsibilities. She, therefore, harboured the idea of providing good education to her daughter. When her daughter completed school education, her husband started to suggest that she be discontinued from studies and married off. Augustine put her foot down, and declared that she would provide education whatever may be the consequences. Her husband also became adamant and declared that he would not support her (both financially and in other respects) in admitting the daughter into the college. Augustine discussed the matter with group members, obtained a loan to admit her in the college and has been supporting her in education only through her own earnings. When this was being discussed, Augustine's husband was also there, and was still defending his position.

It is in this context that, the perception of up to what age boys and girls should be sent to schools and colleges become important. Between 78 and 81 per cent of the women belonging to member and comparison groups stated that they would like to send girls up to 10th class, i.e., up to the age of 14-15 years (Table 5.19). None of the women in either of the two groups stated that girls would be sent to pursue their education as per their wish and will. This was strikingly different in so far as the statements on boys were concerned (Table 5.20). Most of the members stated that the boys could pursue education according to their wish and up to the time that they could obtain job.

Table 5.18 : Reasons for sending children to school (the project area of Sanghamitra)

Reasons	Member group (%)	Comparison group (%)
To get employment	54.72	59.26
Awareness	15.09	14.81
Literacy	16.98	7.41
Do not know	7.55	3.70
Not stated	5.66	14.81
Total (no.)	53	27

Table 5.19 : Perceptions on up to what age should girls study in the project area of Sanghamitra

Responses	Member group (%)	Comparison group (%)
< 14 years	3.77	7.41
14-18 years	81.13	77.78
19-21 years	11.32	14.81
According to their will and interest	0.00	0.00
Do not know	3.77	0.00
Total (no.)	53	27

Table 5.20 : Perceptions on up to what age should boys study in the project area of Sanghamitra

Respons	Member group (%)	Comparison group (%)
14-20 years	13	19
21-30 years	13	7
According to their will and interest	56	63
Until they complete the studies	9	4
Do not know	9	7
Total (no.)	53	27

Participation in Political Institutions in the Project Area of Sanghamitra

The information on whether SHG membership had made any difference to their perceptions on and participation in political institutions in the project area of Sanghamitra is analysed below.

Almost all the women belonging to both groups were participating in the electoral process but a majority of them were aware for which political body did they cast their votes (Table 5.21). About 38 per cent of the women from the member group stated that they listened to radio or watched TV for obtaining news as against only 4 per cent of women in the comparison group. Interestingly, nearly 72 per cent of the women from the comparison group could tell the name of the Chief Minister, while 15 per cent could tell the names of both the Prime Minister and the Chief Minister. The corresponding proportions in the case of women in the comparison group were low at 55 and 4 per cent, respectively. About 6 per cent of the women in the member group thought of contesting for the gram panchayat as against none in the case of the comparison group. A majority of the women stated that women coming to power would help them as they understood the gender issues much better than men.

Table 5.21 : Comparison between members and non-members with regard to political participation (the project area of Sanghamitra)

	Member group (%)	Comparison group (%)
A. Did you vote in the recent election		
Yes	100.00	100.00
No	0.00	0.00
Total (no)	53	27
B. If yes, which election?		
Panchayat	9.43	3.70
Assembly	13.21	11.11
Parliament	1.89	3.70
Assembly & Parliament	3.77	0.00
Panchayat & Parliament	1.89	0.00
Assembly & Panchayat	3.77	3.70
Do not Know	64.15	74.07
Mandal	1.89	3.70
Total (no)	53	27

Conclusions

An analysis of the economic benefits of micro-finance programmes on members of SHGs reveals that the condition of households in the member group was better than those in the comparison group in the following respects :

- The households in the member group had access to credit facility.
- The households in the member group were different from those in the comparison group in terms of total amount saved and number of savings forms used.
- As far as acquisition of productive assets was concerned, a relatively larger proportion of households from the member group had acquired assets such as livestock and land as compared to those in the comparison group.
- Most of the households in the member group had access to more than two livelihood sources as compared to those in the comparison group.
- Most of the households in the member group obtained more than Rs. 20,000 of income in a year. On the other hand, a relatively larger proportion of households from the comparison group obtained less than Rs. 20,000 of annual income.
- The higher income in the case of member households had a favourable impact on the acquisition of consumer durables and expenditure on food, education and health.
- While there were significant economic benefits for members of micro-finance groups, the social benefits seems to be marginal. The decision-making was mostly confined to small and large purchases for the household, self and children. A majority of the women, even after years of membership in the group, did not participate in the decision-making relating to house repair, purchase of land, productive assets, education of boys and girls, etc., as these areas were considered to be the domains of men in the household.

The educational levels of the household members in the case of member group were substantially better than those in the comparison group. However, a significant proportion of women from both the groups stated that girls should be married soon after they attained puberty. Most of the women from both member and comparison groups stated that they would give unlimited freedom for boys to pursue their education. It, therefore, appears that the societal expectations on the age at which girls are to be married, whether women can undertake salaried employment or whether the girl should go to school or not are determined by the parental decision. This is a very well known position and is applicable to women belonging to the member group as well. The obvious conclusion is that the SHG membership has not made any significant difference to the value attached to children's education (especially girls). The observed differences in school attendance between member and comparison groups are to be, therefore, attributed to factors other than the micro-finance.

Years of membership in micro-finance groups has made only marginal difference in so far as the participation of women in the political institutions, and their awareness on who were important political leaders at the time of the survey. In this respect, the women in the comparison group from the project area of Sanghamitra were relatively better. But, it is not clear to what extent this can be attributed to generally higher levels of awareness in Krishna district or to micro-finance groups. The qualitative evidence on participation in political institutions indicates that the SHG membership had not really contributed to gaining awareness on rights that the women had and how to utilize these rights.

6

Attempts at Poverty Reduction by Local Organisations

Introduction

In each of the villages, an organisational mapping was conducted with different focus groups from each of the localities. The mapping exercise sought to obtain information on different local organisations present in the village, and their performance in terms of accountability, transparency, equity and effectiveness. In general, four types of local organisations were mentioned in the mapping exercises. These were line departments, gram panchayat, banks and NGOs. With regard to line departments, the villagers mentioned the schemes operated by them. While the contribution of NGOs has been discussed in the previous chapter, this chapter takes up the role of development actors other than the NGOs in the project areas of SHARE and Sanghamitra, respectively.

Role of Development Actors—The Project Area of SHARE

Line Departments

The line departments/ministries at Central, State, district and lower levels undertake agricultural and rural development programmes[1] to address the problems of the poor, viz., assetlessness, unemployment, poverty and inability to meet the basic needs.

Most of the people in the selected villages were aware of programmes relating to basic needs. All the sample households utilised the PDS to obtain rice and other essential provisions. Most of them had availed housing facilities from the government. They were aware of pensions given to the old and widows, and also the procedures involved; a significant proportion of them had even obtained them. Another government programme that was often utilised was assistance provided to educate girl children. In addition, most of the sample households utilised health and educational facilities within the villages. One significant aspect was that there was no difference in the utilisation pattern between the NGO villages and Melvallam. The following were the difficulties faced by the poor in obtaining benefits from the government.

'Corruption' in the line departments was one the often cited factor. Even those poor who had obtained benefits had to bribe the concerned officials. For instance, one widow obtains Rs.150 as pension every month. She had to spend an amount almost equivalent to six months of pension as bribes to doctor, officials in the line department, travel and documentation.

The demand for housing facility was quite high in the selected villages. The Government has been providing housing facility for the last 15 years. Now-a-days, it has become difficult to mobilise assistance towards housing because of widespread perception among government officials that this need has already been met. To some extent this view has been strengthened by incidents of following type. About 20 per cent of our sample households, who had already obtained housing facility from the government, either did not stay in these houses (rented out) or sold away these houses as they had already had their own houses. In a few cases, the 'request' for housing came from those households which wanted an additional house for future requirement such as unmarried son in the household might be in need of house when he got married.

Realising that obtaining assistance towards housing was becoming difficult, forty SC households in Sabthalipuram (a few of them wanted an additional house) joined together to approach the government officials and to undertake collective follow-up. They contributed money towards expenditure on travel and other expenses of three representatives. After five years, a few of the households obtained benefits. This had both positive and negative consequences for future collective action. Positive consequence was that some of the needy households could obtain housing facility through collective action. The negative consequence was that there were criticisms on the accountability of the representatives. Some members of this group noted that collective action would not work in the case of obtaining loans (as the banks would like the representatives to take up repayment responsibility). It could, however, work if the nature of assistance was grant or the one which benefited a cross-section of the poor households in the village.

Some of the households could not utilise the government schemes and programmes because of their values and attitudes. One member of craft centre thought of applying for old age pension for her father-in-law. Although she was aware of the procedures, she did not approach the concerned officials because she had to tell them that the old man did not have any relatives. This was difficult for her. Others stated that corruption, cumbersome procedures and bureaucratic delays came in the way of obtaining these benefits.

To conclude, the widespread perception among the poor was that the line departments did not have pro-poor orientation, inefficient in the selection of the needy and in the provision of benefits. They also stated that the government officials were corrupt and insisted on countless procedures. The perception among government officials was that the very poor were not organised to obtain enduring benefits from the government. Hence, the non-poor and middlemen were the ones who obtained government benefits as the government officials faced difficulties and constraints in obtaining proper information on the poor in the process of implementation. Thus, line departments spent vast sums of money on rural development and poverty alleviation; but, the very poor failed to benefit from this expenditure.

Banks and Cooperatives

The Formal Rural Banking System (FRBS)[2] has had phenomenal expansion in the number of bank branches (especially in rural areas), deposits and quantum of advances. In order to improve access to credit for the rural poor, commercial banks were asked to play a social role, and to target credit through a number of subsidised credit programmes. The FRBS was also made responsible for disbursing loans to beneficiaries of Integrated Rural Development Programme (IRDP) and Development of Women and Children in Rural Areas (DWCRA) programmes in collaboration with the line departments, and elected leaders of gram panchayats. IRDP was initiated on a nationwide basis in the early 1980s to increase the income generating assets of the poor directly through a mixture of subsidies and credit. Under DWCRA programme, government staff in a village would form a 15-member women's group, which, after regular savings of Rs. 30 by each of the members for six months, would be eligible for an interest-free loan from a local formal bank. The number of DWCRA groups increased phenomenally in the recent years (Rajakutty 1997: 91).

All the three villages are served by commercial banks and cooperatives. Each of the commercial banks in these villages has mobilised Rs. 15-20 million as deposits, and lent about Rs. 10-12 million as credit. In each of the credit cooperatives, the proportion of the borrowing members is less than 50 per cent; and the share capital forms only a small proportion of the total lending. Hence, they depend on the apex cooperative bank for on-lending. The credit cooperatives have mobilised Rs. 3.5-6 million as deposits, and have devoted Rs. 2-8 million for rural lending.

From the official standpoint, these financial institutions have been doing very well. It is to be noted that the FRBS was in crisis during 1980s with mounting overdues (largely due to structural, managerial and political factors) and recurring losses. As part of the ongoing financial reforms (linked to structural adjustment policies), banks were asked to follow strict credit norms, and earn profits every year. In the past, the performance of the branch manager was evaluated on the basis of deposits. Now, the criteria is lending, recovery and profits in addition to deposit mobilisation. The managers of the commercial banks and credit cooperatives in the selected villages have fulfilled the criteria, and are in the good books of the management. This is incredible because, amongst other reasons, the losses in the past were attributed to priority sector lending[3]. The information from banks in the selected villages shows that they provided over 80 per cent of the credit to priority sector; yet, they achieved profits. How was this possible?

The answer to this lies in lending portfolio. The distribution of total advances shows that a bulk of the amount (90 per cent in the case of cooperatives and 75 per cent in the case of commercial banks) went for crop production, which fell under the priority sector. But, a disaggregation of the amount lent for crop production shows that loans against jewellery and deposits accounted for a large proportion of the amount. A significant proportion of the amount was given for sugarcane cultivation with security provided by the local sugar factory. The rest of the amount was given to farmers directly. Even here also, 70 per cent were old borrowers, having regular contact with the banks. Thus, a bulk of the loan amount was given to those who provided individual security (jewellery and deposits), or through sugar factory. The rest of the amount was also secured in the sense that only the regularly repaying borrowers were given credit.

Given that the poor and poorest in the selected villages did not have landed assets, jewellery and deposits, it is obvious that much of the credit from FRBS was going to the well-off and better-off. Then, how about credit for poverty alleviation?

The financial institutions in the village provide only 5 to 10 per cent of the total advances in a year to IRDP, employment generation and DWCRA. The reasons attributed to lower allocation of funds for poverty alleviation were the following; first, the loans given for poverty alleviation suffered from problems of selection, monitoring and repayment. Second, the beneficiaries were selected by line departments and elected leaders of gram panchayats. It was alleged that under considerations of political patronage, and corruption, they selected wrong beneficiaries. Hence, the list sent by the line departments and local decentralised government was looked into with suspicion. In fact, the financial institutions rejected a large number of applications by giving some reason or the other. Third, the branch managers were advised by the regional offices to go slow as far as lending for poverty alleviation was concerned. They were asked not to lend any amount more than what was fixed as target for each bank branch.

The manager of the local bank branch at Mottupalayam acknowledged that they were not doing anything for poverty alleviation leave alone reduction. He noted that certain conditions were essential if banks were to play a significant role in poverty alleviation: (i) there needed to be appropriate legal provisions for recovering the loans; (ii) the selection of borrowers should be left to the banks; (iii) if (ii) was not possible, the line departments and elected members of gram panchayats should also be involved in recovery.

He concluded that these conditions were difficult to be achieved in the short-run. Hence the NGOs might have to shoulder greater responsibility of poverty alleviation.

People perceived banks to be difficult institutions to gain access. When asked about the possibility of approaching banks for loan towards poverty alleviation, a deserted woman stated that 'even men (with literacy, wider contacts and mobility) cannot access the credit from banks: how, I can do that'. The widespread perception was that banks did not lend to the poor, insisted on countless procedural formalities, asked for collateral security, etc. Hence, unless recommended by an influential person (landlord, politician, middlemen), it was difficult to access the credit from banks for poverty alleviation.

Decentralised Government

The need for micro-level institutional arrangement to involve the people in formulation, implementation and monitoring of the programmes was felt soon after the independence. Based on the recommendations of the Balvantrai Committee, the Panchayat Raj Institutions (PRIs) were introduced to enable the participation of disadvantaged groups of women, *dalits* and *adivasis*. The studies on the experience of PRIs in several states, however, show that the participation of the rural masses in micro planning was minimal[4]. As a result, the decentralised structure in the form of a 'four pillar state', resting on the foundations of a four-fold sharing of power between the village, the district, state and the centre, and bringing about a people-centered rural development remained more in the realm of an idea than in the practice.

Following the report of the Asoka Mehta Committee, and the experiences of West Bengal and Karnataka[5] states in decentralised governance, the discussion on how to secure people's participation in the development process through PRIs and devolution of powers continued. The discussion was also influenced by the world-wide debate on the need to involve the people in their own development. The aid agencies, multi-lateral and bilateral, have also stressed the need to revitalise PRIs to secure people's participation in the development process. Subsequently, the Indian government brought in the 73rd Constitutional Amendment in 1993. The Amendment made key changes in the rules relating to decentralised government[6] and gave priority to decentralisation, people's participation and democracy at the local level. The Amendment adopted a three-tier model with democratically elected governments at the village, taluk or mandal and district levels. The gram sabha (people's assembly) consisting of all voters in a gram panchayat area was to be convened at least twice a year at the ward level to incorporate people's views into planning and implementation.

The Tamil Nadu state did not hold elections to gram panchayats for a long time. With 73rd Constitutional Amendment, the state government had to conduct the elections in 1996. The target group of SHARE did not contest to any of the positions in Sabthalipuram and Mottupalayam. In all the three villages, gram panchayats were constituted in 1996.

The president of the gram panchayat, in which Sabthalipuram is a part, was elected in 1995. She is a graduate, and belongs to Vanniyar caste. She won the post which was contested by six persons. When asked about what image she had on Sabthalipuram, she noted that, 'the village predominantly consists of Vanniyars who solidly stood behind me in the election'. Interestingly, she did not get the image of silted tanks, poor sanitation, over 50 per cent of the poor, and unemployed in the village. When asked, what has been done to the poor in the village, she looked very baffled. She posed a question:

'What has gram panchayat to do with poverty?'

This question naturally surprised us. But, provided answer to several questions. The 73rd Constitutional Amendment may have provided political opportunity, but not succeeded in making poor as political agency, and poverty as a concern. The President was articulating the perception of many people (both elected leaders of gram panchayats and rural poor) on gram panchayat that it was 'an elected executive to implement public works'. It was not perceived as an organisation which would enable the participation of the poor so that they could access, control and contest policy formulation and implementation.

This is corroborated by the following. An analysis of income and expenditure of gram panchayats in the selected villages shows that a bulk of the expenditure incurred in the last two years was on protected water supply, road construction and providing (and maintenance of) street lights. The gram sabhas were not held even once to ascertain the views of the people in planning, implementation and monitoring of the programmes. It is generally noted that the presidents of gram panchayats were busy in recovering vast sums spent during the elections by awarding contracts for those offering heavy cuts, and those who had supported them in the elections. The ward members (belonging to political parties other than to which the presidents belong) complained about the corrupt practices of presidents. Yet, as on date, they had done nothing to raise these issues in gram panchayat meetings, except questioning the choice of person to whom the contract was awarded.

Poverty alleviation is to some extent done by the gram panchayats. Works relating to Protected Water supply and sanitation contribute to improvement of health status. They participate in the selection of beneficiaries for IRDP, widow pension scheme, incentives for girl education, etc. While the presidents complain about lack of absolute powers in the selection, the perception of the people is that the selection is based on political consideration and corruption. The presidents refuted the allegations by stating that they strictly went by the list of the poor prepared for each of the villages. When a copy of the list was requested to be made available to us, it was stated that the list was not readily available. Our repeated visits proved to be futile as far as obtaining the list was concerned.

To conclude, the 73rd Amendment provided an opportunity to the poor to occupy executive positions in the local decentralised government, and control policy formulation and implementation. But, the widespread perception among both the elected leaders and poor is that the mandate of local decentralised government is to implement public works rather that to enable the poor to access and control policy formulation and implementation in their favour.

Role of Development Actors in the Project Area of Sanghamitra

Line Departments

The frequently mentioned schemes in the organisational mapping were public distribution system, SC/ST corporation schemes, land *pattas* for house sites, programmes relating to old age pension, free education, hostel and *bhagya jyothi*. Most of the members in SHGs are aware of public distribution system, regularly avail and utilise the subsidised foodgrains provided by the civil supplies department. In all the villages, they have ranked this to be very important and significant in terms of effectiveness and equity. Only a few of the households were aware of free sites for house construction and programmes relating to OAP, free education and hostel facilities.

The members in SHGs could access these programmes somewhat easily as compared to non-member households in Bathinapadu and Kothapeta and all the households in S. Amarvaram. The SHG members utilised the SHG as an organisation to put pressure on the government officials. Whenever they had problem with regard to these schemes and programmes, they approached either the NGO staff or went to the offices collectively to ask for these schemes. As a result, the benefits accrued to the members seem to be significantly better than those to non-member households. For instance, in all the villages, the member households had availed housing schemes, obtained DWCRA support (revolving fund to the group) and a few of them also obtained old age pension. A majority of the sample members stated that they did not pay any bribe although they were asked for it. Only four member households stated that they paid bribe to the government officials and middlemen.

On the other hand, the non-member household faced many problems in obtaining housing and other schemes. The reason for this, it was stated in organisational mapping, that they did not have an organisation representing them. To a question why they did not then join in SHG or formed their own group, the response was the participation in these groups was costly in terms of time and payment of regular savings. They, however, noted that they regularly obtained provisions from the PDS.

All the households, irrespective of whether they were in SHGs or not, noted that the hospital and educational facilities were ineffective. The main reasons for this were irregular visits by doctors and teachers, lack of supply of medicines, widespread perception that the medicines supplied by the PHC were ineffective in curing the illness, etc. Further, the free hostel facility was utilised by a number of households. However, the drop-out of children from these hostels was a frequent problem because of poor living conditions in the hostels, prevalence of wage labour market for children and the widespread perception that the educated often found it difficult to obtain jobs.

However, one did not find any evidence that the households collectively approached either the hospital or hostel authorities to press for improvement in these facilities. The reasons cited by the villagers were that they did not have time. Further, the limited and insecure livelihoods also came in the way of these households spending their time on collective action. More plausible reason was that since this was not private good, and not all the households were interested in the improvement of these facilities (the better-off in these villages do not demand the services provided education and health department), the collective action was non-existent.

Banks and Credit Co-operatives

The villages are served both by the commercial banks and credit co-operatives. In the organisational mapping, the banks and co-operatives obtained lower ranks in SC localities, while they were placed at higher position in non-SC localities. The distant location was cited as one of the reasons, but not an important reason. The reasons why SC households assigned lower ranks to these institutions have been discussed below.

- The purpose for which most of the loans from three commercial banks given was the cultivation of cotton crop during the period 1994-1998. Banks considered the crop loans to be secure because these loans were sought by the better-off having considerable extent of land. Further, these households had been obtaining crop loans from banks, and there was an element of trust and familiarity between the bank and borrowers.
- The perception was that the credit co-operatives gave loans mainly to the landed. They did not give any loans to the landless poor.
- Since most of the poor and poorest did not have land, they required credit for allied and non-farm activities such as purchase of milch animals, petty shops, rickshaw, sewing machine, laundry, etc. However, the proportion of total credit given for these activities was 27 per cent for all the

households in Bathinapadu village during the period 1994-1998. The proportion was even less at 17 per cent in Kothapeta village. Thus, the landless households belonging to SC community did not perceive that the banks were really helpful to them.

- Most of these loans were provided to the better-off belonging to non-SC communities. Hence, this was the reason why the households in non-SC localities assigned higher rank to the banks and cooperatives.
- The poor, in general felt that they kept approaching the bank; but, they were not provided with credit. Further, they also stated that the bankers' attitude was indifferent and abusive. They also stated that they approached the president of gram panchayat in this regard. His intervention was not much of use.

The perceptions of bankers and gram panchayat president were somewhat different. According to the branch manager of a commercial bank, the root cause for poverty was laziness. He noted that whenever he visited a village, he would come across a large number of young and old men who would not have gone for work. According to the bank manager, there was plenty of work available and the landowners in fact were facing the problem of shortage of workers. He further stated that in the context of widespread availability of work and higher wages for agricultural labour, people not going for work could not be excused. Because the laziness was the principal reason for poverty, the poor could not productively utilise the credit even if bank gave them credit. Hence, there was no need to give loans for income generation or poverty alleviation.

He also noted that a majority of the poor households obtained IRDP loans in the past, and they did not repay their loans. Hence, they could not be given any fresh loans until they repaid the old loans. This was the perception that was shared by the president of the gram panchayat also.

Gram Panchayat

The discussions with the people in focus group interviews and gram panchayat members revealed the following:

- A majority of the members got elected to the gram panchayat through contest, and they had to spend considerable amount for the election. The president of one gram panchayat stated that he spent Rs.40,000 on election.
- The meetings were not regularly held. In one of the villages, the gram panchayat meeting was not held in 1997 and 1998. The minutes of the meeting were, nevertheless, prepared and signatures were obtained.
- The gram panchayats had limited resources at their disposal. All of them depended on state and central government transfers, and local resource mobilisation was insignificant. Even the user fees for drinking water was not mobilised.
- With government transfers, all the panchayats were undertaking the works relating to water and sanitation, and road construction.
- These works were normally sanctioned to ward members or their relatives for construction. The perception of the villagers was that the contractors were making money in the process.

In general, the perception was that the gram panchayat was not meant for direct poverty alleviation. This was hardly surprising that although the panchayat could have incorporated the concerns of the poor such as providing work to those who have enrolled themselves as unemployed, there was no evidence to this effect. Hence, in many localities, the people did not even remember the gram panchayat as one of the organisations which alleviated their poverty. Only after a reminder from the facilitator did they discuss the poverty alleviation component of the gram panchayat.

Conclusions

The main causes of poverty, according to the people were lack of assets (land) and unemployment. The poverty alleviation programmes that were being carried out by the local organisations had the potential to address these problems. But, the evidence points out that the programmes were mainly related to PDS, OAP and some bank loans. These would not remove the main causes of poverty. Further, banks did not provide credit for income generation or asset building. The programmes of gram panchayat were essentially related to building the infrastructure in the village, and they did not incorporate the concerns of the poor. Thus, there was no clear congruence between the situation of the poor and poverty alleviation programmes undertaken by the local organisations.

Notes

1. For a critical review of these programmes, see, Rajasekhar and Namerta (1994).
2. Consists of commercial banks, RRBs and cooperatives.
3. The FRBS has stipulated from the mid-1980s that 40 per cent of the total advances made by the commercial banks, RRBs and cooperatives should go for agriculture, small manufacturing, trades and services. This is referred to as priority sector lending.
4. This was because of the politicisation of PRIs : dominant role played by the vested interests in rural areas, corruption, inadequate devolution of powers and responsibilities to PRIs, frequent interference by the bureaucracy, irregular elections to PRIs, etc.
5. For an analysis of the Karnataka experiment, see, Aziz (1993).
6. The Amendment incorporated the following mandatory rules to secure people's participation in PRIs: (i) elections to PRIs are to be held regularly (and at the village level on non-political party symbols); (ii) reservation of seats for women, *dalits* and *adivasis* in PRIs at all levels; (iii) mandatory elections after completing five-year term; (iv) mandatory constitution of a Finance Commission once in five years to review the finances and to recommend the size of funds to be allocated to the panchayats and also the principles and the basis on which taxes should be collected in panchayat areas; (v) PRIs are made responsible to implement the government schemes and programmes aimed at economic development and social justice in rural areas; and (vi) the responsibility of collecting taxes is placed with the panchayats.

7

Strategies Adopted by the Poor

Introduction

What strategies do the poor adopt to cope with poverty? Table 7.1 provides the responses of persons belonging to very poor and poor categories in the focus group interview conducted in all the villages from Andhra Pradesh. The participants in the meeting were not in a position to give ranks to the strategies that they adopted. Hence, they were encouraged to come up with three categories (critical, very important and important) of strategies.

Hiring themselves out as wage labourers and participation in *mutah* labour were considered to be critical in all the SC localities in the selected villages. On the other hand, these two were not considered to be critical by the poor from the localities of upper castes. In fact, wage labour was considered to be just important in the upper caste locality of S. Amaravaram, while *mutah* labour did not even figure here. This was because the poor from upper caste localities perceived the involvement in non-farm activities as critical strategy, while rearing livestock animals as very important strategy. As the discussion on causes of poverty also suggested they had not stated the problem of lack of capital to undertake non-farm activities is an important one. Other important strategies were leasing in land and savings in self-help groups, which enabled the poor to borrow to meet the consumption credit needs and to start small income generation activities. The dependence on the Public Distribution System (PDS) was also considered to be very important strategy by the poor from SC localities of Bathinapadu and Kothapeta. It might be mentioned here that the Andhra Pradesh government had been following a pro-poor oriented PDS since 1983 under which rice was supplied at very subsidised rates. The poor from the SC locality of Kothapeta also mentioned child labour, out-migration and kind savings as important strategies to cope with poverty. The strategy of borrowing from moneylenders to meet consumption needs was followed by the poor in the SC locality of S. Amaravaram because, unlike the other two villages, well-functioning self-help groups in micro-finance did not exist in this village.

Table 7.1 : Strategies followed by the poor to cope with poverty across the selected villages

Particulars	Bathinapadu	Kothapeta		S.Amaravaram	
		SCs	Others	SCs	Others
Depending on wage labour	***	***	**	***	*
Mutah labour	***	***	*	***	
Rearing of milch animals, sheep and chicken	*	*	**	*	**
Saving in self-help groups	**	*	*		
Leasing in land	*	*	*	**	
Non-farm activities	*	**	***	*	***
Child labour		**			
Kitchen gardening		*			
Out-migration		**			
Kind savings	**	*			
Dependence on public distribution system	**	**			
Borrowing from money lenders				**	
Working as housemaids in the households belonging to upper castes				**	
Purchase of land					*

Note: *** Critical; ** Very important; * Important
Source: Focus group interviews in the selected villages.

The above discussion suggests that a large proportion of households across the selected villages lived in poverty, which was mainly caused by lack of assets. With landlessness, the only option left to them was wage labour. But, the poor in the selected villages could obtain sufficient and secure wage income due to uncertain agricultural labour market. Faced with this kind of situation, the poor adopted several strategies to cope with poverty, which were different between the SC households and others in the selected villages. The poor from upper castes and artisan castes adopted individual strategies of undertaking income generating activities such as rearing of livestock animals, petty business, services (renting out of agricultural equipment, hotels, etc). On the other hand, the poor from all the SC localities adopted wage labour as a critical strategy. Further, they seemed to be adopting *mutah* labour as an organising practice to come to terms with uncertain agricultural labour market. In this context, there is need to discuss the importance of *mutah* labour for the agricultural labour households.

Importance of *Mutah* Labour

Agricultural Labour Households (ALHs) constitute about 30 per cent of the total households in India (28 per cent of the total rural population) and account for 38 per cent of the total rural population in absolute poverty and about 60 per cent of total unemployed person-days in rural India. The incidence of poverty among ALHs is about 63 per cent. Thus ALHs are clearly the most poverty-stricken group in India.

Casual labour, mostly daily wage, is the most common contractual form of agricultural wage labour. There has been a significant trend towards casualisation of wage labour in the last couple of decades or so[1]. The agricultural labour market (especially for causal labourers) is characterised by conditions of excess supply. Involuntary unemployment among agricultural labourers is both persisting and substantial (Datt 1996). The real wages of agricultural labourers, which were declining until the mid-1970s, increased during the period 1977-78 to 1987-88 (Vaidyanathan 1994), and were marked by year-to-year fluctuations after the introduction of the New Economic Policy in 1991 largely because of increased prices of essential commodities.

The government programmes, introduced to improve the condition of the agricultural labourers, have not been successful. The land reforms measures aimed at redistribution of land among the landless and providing secured tenancy rights to the poor tenants have failed in achieving their objectives. The employment-oriented programmes such as National Rural Employment Programme and Jawahar Rozgar Yojana have provided employment to the rural poor reporting unemployment; but, the employment provision was not sustained. The government sought to implement minimum wages to the agricultural labourers; but, the wages paid to the labourers were far below than those fixed by the government.

Thus, the agricultural labour households face problems of unemployment, casualisation of labour, poverty and inability to obtain enduring benefits from the government programmes. What will the ALHs do when they are faced with poverty? What strategies do they adopt to cope with poverty? Given that employment and wages determine the economic condition of the labourers, what strategies do they adopt to secure their interests in the labour market? The literature suggests that the labourers adopt the following strategies.

It is frequently noted that the labourers borrow from the cultivator-cum-moneylenders to meet the consumption needs especially during the slack season with an implicit (or explicit) understanding that the former works for the latter during the peak season at wages less than those ruling in the market (Rudra 1982). Such inter-linkages between credit and labour markets also figure in the attached labourer arrangements. Although the studies highlight the adverse impact of interlocking of credit and labour markets on agricultural labourers, the borrowing from cultivator-cum-money lenders is perceived by labourers as a strategy to tide over the shortfalls in consumption during the slack season. The recent evidence, however, shows that the phenomenon of interlocked credit and labour markets is mostly confined to the attached labour system, and to east India (Datt 1996).

The second strategy adopted by ALHs is migration to agriculturally prosperous regions. A well-known example is the permanent migration of labourers from the backward state of Bihar to agriculturally developed states of Punjab and Haryana. Seasonal migration is also reported from most of the provinces in India; the labourers annually migrate to the neighbouring agriculturally prosperous regions during the slack seasons and come back to their own villages when agricultural operations are about to commence.

Yet, another strategy of ALHs is to diversify their employment portfolio. The studies note that, in addition to wage labour, ALHs are involved in leasing in land, livestock rearing and non-farm activities[2]. The last activity seems to be the most chosen strategy for the ALHs to cope with poverty. It appears that, poverty and unemployment (both seasonal and disguised) force ALHs to take up non-farm activities as supplementary and complementary livelihood activities (Vaidyanathan 1986; Unni 1991). In fact, the puzzling feature of rising real wages coexisting with high incidence of unemployment was explained through non-farm activities tightening the labour market, and thereby, pushing the real wages up (Bhalla 1993; Sen 1996).

The strategy of agricultural labourers coming together in a formal union to fight for their rights relating to employment, wages and minimum needs seems to be confined to a few states, the notable among them being West Bengal and Kerala. In all the other states, the formal unions of agricultural labourers exist, but, do not effectively represent the interests of agricultural labourers (Kannan 1993).

One of the less-documented strategies that the ALHs adopt is to participate in the labour market through *mutah*[3] labour. Under this, a group of labourers along with *maestri*[4] (supervisor) takes up agricultural work either on the basis of piece-meal rate or on the basis of daily wage rate. The discussions with heads of labour unions reveal that they regard this as the best practice for agricultural labourers to secure employment and higher wages.

This chapter seeks to discuss and analyse the evolution, functioning and performance of the *mutah* labour with the help of data collected only from Andhra village. The database is mapping of poverty and local organisation in three villages and information collected from 56 sample farm labourers, 14 *maestris* and 15 ryots by using a structured questionnaire.

Evolution of *Mutah* Labour

The number of agricultural labour *mutahs* varied from 4 in Bathinapadu and 8 each in Kothapeta and S. Amaravaram. Of the 20 *mutahs* in three villages, 14 were selected for an intensive analysis. The information on the year of inception from 14 *maestris* shows that one *mutah* had emerged before 1970, while five of them were formed between 1970 and 1986. As many as eight *mutahs* were formed during the period 1987 to 1996 (Table 7.2). Thus, the *mutah* labour in the selected villages was there even before 1970, and gained momentum in late 1980s and 1990s.

Table 7.2 : Distribution of the selected *Mutahs* by year of inception and number of labourers

Period	Distribution of *mutahs* by size				
	<10	11 to 20	21 to 30	31 and above	Total
Before 1970	1				1
1970 to 1986		3	2		5
1986 to 1996		5	2	1	8
Total	1	8	4	1	14

Source: Survey data.

What factors contributed to the growth of *mutah* labour practice? The responses of *maestris* who formed *mutah* in 1970s shows that ryots themselves suggested them to form a *mutah*. According to these *maestris*, the ryots were aware of the existence of *mutah* labour in the neighbouring Guntur district, where they were essentially confined to tobacco crop especially in the activity of curing of tobacco leaves. These *mutahs* were in the news by mid 1960s as they constantly fought with tobacco companies for higher wages, and were occasionally involved in strikes (Duvvury 1999). Then, why did the ryots suggest the formation of *mutahs* might go against their interests?

Spread of Irrigation and New Agricultural Technology

An answer to this question can be found in the spread of irrigation and introduction of new agricultural technology in the locality. Prior to 1960s, much of the cultivation was rain-fed in these villages. With the advent of oil and electricity engines and spread of lift-irrigation technology, the irrigated area started spreading. By 1970s, the farmers also started to draw irrigation water from the Krishna river, and from the canal network of Nagarjuna Sagar dam.

This resulted in an intensification of the commercialised agriculture. Though commercial crops such as cotton, groundnut, chillies and tobacco were cultivated around 1960s, cereals such as jowar and bajra were the important crops in the cropping pattern. With the availability of irrigation water, the area under coarse cereals was replaced by paddy and the commercial crops. Further, the farmers began to use irrigation water for the cultivation of commercial crops. This enabled them to introduce the high yielding varieties of paddy, groundnut, cotton and chillies. There was also a rapid rise in the consumption of chemical fertilisers.

With the spread of irrigation, new agricultural technology and intensified commercial agriculture, the demand for labour went up. So much so that children, who were not allowed by the farmers to work in the fields, began to be recruited into the workforce as the demand for labour started to increase. With reduced time gap between the crops, and agricultural operations going on simultaneously in more than one plot, the farmers found it difficult to supervise the work of labourers. Added to that, if a ryot had to engage 20 labourers for agricultural work, he had to visit 20 different houses to call them. All these factors influenced the farmers to entrust the responsibility of bringing a group of labourers, and supervising their work to a person who was known to them or who was regularly working for them. Such persons gradually became *mutah maestris*.

Feminisation of Agricultural Labour Market

Another factor contributing to the development of *mutah* labour was the feminisation of labour. Around 1950s, the involvement of men in the agricultural labour market was relatively more. They were mainly engaged in clearing the bushes, deep ploughing, transporting the manure to the fields, preparing the soil for cultivation, sowing, cultivation, harvesting, transporting the produce to the houses of ryots, etc. On the other hand, women were mainly engaged in weeding, and plucking of greengram and cotton

With the introduction of new agricultural technology and government policies on mechanisation, the ryots started to go for tractors, harvesters and threshers, which, according to one labourer, "are there everywhere (now in the villages)". The impact of mechanisation on employment opportunities was selective in the sense that it progressively reduced the employment opportunities for men. Another aspect was that, with relatively higher wages in non-farm activities such as quarrying and better earnings in petty business and small trading, the male agricultural labourers started to gradually move out of the agricultural labour market. This contributed to the growing demand for male agricultural labourers. This further induced the ryots to vigorously pursue the mechanisation policy. Even if a ryot could not afford to buy a machine on his own, the development of rental market for machinery contributed to the mechanisation process.

The rapid mechanisation process in the selected villages did not affect the female employment opportunities. Transplantation, weeding, plucking of cotton, greengram and groundnut, and plucking and grading of tobacco leaves continued to be done with human labour. As female agricultural labourers were supposed to undertake these operations traditionally, they continued to have employment within agriculture. Thus, female workers started to dominate the agricultural labour market.

This is further corroborated by the primary data on distribution of workers by activities in the ALHs. Of the 170 workers from 56 sample ALHs, 86 were male workers and 84 were female workers. Of the 84 female workers, over 90 per cent had reported wage work in agriculture as their main occupation, while the rest had reported that the activities that combined wage work with non-farm employment and cultivation as principal occupation (Table 7.3). In contrast, of the 86 male workers, only 43 per cent had reported wage work in agriculture as the principal occupation. For about 30 per cent, non-farm activities were the main occupation, while a combination of farm and non-farm activities was the principal

Table 7.3 : Distribution of workers from the sample ALHs by their principal occupation

Activities	Male workers (%) participating in the labour market			Female workers (%) participating in the labour market		
	Through *Mutah*	As individuals	Total	Through *Mutah*	As individuals	Total
Agricultural labour	65.4	8.8	43.0	98.7	0.0	90.5
Non-farm activities	9.6	61.8	30.2	0.0	42.9	3.6
Cultivation, farm and non-farm work	0.0	20.6	8.2	0.0	57.1	4.8
Agricultural labour and non-farm activities	25.0	8.8	18.6	1.3	0.0	1.1
Total (no.)	52	34	86	77	7	84

Source : Survey Data.

source of livelihood for the rest. The discussions with the labourers reveal that the male workers temporarily withdrew from non-farm activities during the peak agricultural seasons as wage rates in agriculture were relatively higher during this season.

The feminisation of agricultural labour market contributed to further growth of *mutahs*—especially those headed by a woman and consisting of only female workers. This was because the *mutah*, as we shall discuss further below, was advantageous to female agricultural labourers who would also be involved in domestic chores. Secondly, formation of a *mutah* was considered to be essential to counter the perception of *ryots* that female workers were 'captive labour'. The responses of *maestris* on the factors contributing to the formation also reveals the same; one *maestri*, for instance, stated that the *mutah* was formed because 'bargaining capacity has less in individual labour'.

Uncertainties of Agricultural Labour Market

Notwithstanding the spread of irrigation, intensification of commercial agriculture and new agricultural technology, the agricultural labour market became uncertain in the last fifteen years in the selected villages due to the following reasons. First, the mechanisation process reduced the total quantum of employment available in the locality. Second, a decline in the average size of landholdings in the villages due to higher rates of partitioning among the rich cultivators has had an adverse impact on total employment available as the incidence of family labour was known to be high on small and medium landholdings. Third, with land values increasing[5] and land lease market[6] becoming competitive in the selected villages, the only option left to the ALHs was wage labour in agriculture and non-farm activities. This resulted in excess supply of labourers. Fourth, the practice of ALHs to recruit children into the labour market at an early age and inability to send them to the school also contributed to the excess supply of labourers. All these factors imply that agricultural employment opportunities were available during the peak season, and became uncertain during the slack season. The *mutah*, as we shall discuss below, was helpful in maximising employment opportunities to the existing supply of labourers during the peak season, and provided as much employment as possible during the slack season.

Table 7.1 : When and why labourers joined the *Mutahs*

Year of joining in the group						
Period	Before 1979	1980-84	1985-89	1990-95	1995-98	Total
Number	8	9	10	6	23	56
%	14.3	16.1	17.9	10.7	41.1	100.0
Previous employment and work						
Particulars	Unemployed (housewife)	Attached labour	Casual workers	Others	Total	
Number	14	8	26	8	56	
%	25.0	14.3	46.4	14.3	100.0	
Factors prompting the labourers to join in the ***Mutah***						
Factors	Regular work	Need not search for work	Working in a group is fun	Higher wages & meet the family expenditure	More leisure	Total
Number	13	8	8	18	9	56
%	23.2	14.3	14.3	32.1	16.1	100.0

Source: Primary survey conducted in the selected villages.

The responses of *maestris* and labourers corroborate this. For instance, four out of 14 *maestris* stated that the possibility of finding more employment for their fellow labourers prompted them to form a *mutah*. The information from labourers shows that nearly 70 per cent of them joined in the *mutahs* since 1985 and about 45 per cent were working as casual agricultural wage labourers before joining in the *mutah*. Table 7.4 shows that an important reason for joining in the *mutahs* was regular work availability and they did not have to go in search of work.

Functioning of the *Mutah* Labour

The total number of labourers in each *mutah* varied from 10-35. Eight out of 14 *mutahs* had 10-20 labourers, while four of them had 20-30 labourers (Table 7.2). This, however, did not mean that the total number of labourers in *mutah* remained unchanged in a year. When a particular *mutah* managed to obtain larger work, it recruited labourers from other *mutahs*. But, each of the *maestri* had a group of labourers associated with her/him, and these labourers participated in the labour market through her/him for most part of the year. As of now, the average size of the *mutah* is around 15, while it used to be around 40 about 30 years ago.

Of the 14 *mutahs*. 10 were headed by women. Nine of them consisted of only female workers. In general, female-headed *mutahs* consisted of women or had higher proportion of female workers. However, it should be mentioned that even female *mutahs* also recruited men for certain operations such as transplantation and grading of tobacco (where the payment was usually for a pair consisting man and woman). In such cases, men, mostly relatives of female workers, withdrew from the non-agricultural activities and/ or came from other *mutahs*. There were no *mutahs* consisting of only men in the agricultural labour market[7]. In order to expand the membership both in terms of numbers and male workers to meet the demand for undertaking a particular agricultural operation, each of the *maestris* had cordial relationship and reciprocated with one or two other *mutahs* in the village.

The *mutahs* in Kothapeta and S. Amaravaram undertook work for the ryots in the same village, while those in Bathinapadu in the neighbouring village. In general, there was no bar on undertaking wage work in the neighbouring villages. If offered more wages and transportation facilities, the *mutahs* went to the nearby villages (i.e., which were located 10-15 kms away from their own village). They did not go to distant villages, as this was expensive for ryots who had to bear transportation charges and the invariable time loss in the commutation. Going to other villages did not happen (even if higher wages were offered) in a situation of conflict relating to wages or otherwise between ryots and *mutahs* or labourers in that village.

It was the responsibility of the *maestri* to find work for labourers. During the peak season, the ryots competed with each other in assigning work to a *mutah*. On such occasions, the *mutah* went to work in the highest bidders' field, though past relationships with a particular ryot also came into reckoning at times. During the slack season, the *maestri* went to the ryots in search of work. Some of the *maestris* had managed to develop good relationship with a few ryots, which helped them in finding work for the group.

The *mutahs* undertook activity contract when demand for labourers for that activity was high. The demand for labour reached peak during the transplantation and harvesting of tobacco, chillies, paddy, cotton, greengram and groundnut. The *mutahs* preferred to undertake these activities on piece-meal rate and shared the income equally among them. When a *mutah* undertook an activity contract, the *maestri* ensured that all the labourers were in the field by 6 a.m. and stayed up to 6 p.m. The activity contract did not require much supervision either on the part of *maestri* or the ryot as far as the completion of work was concerned. The ryots, however, supervised the work to ensure that the quality was maintained. The average wage, under activity contract, for men and women, worked out to be Rs. 60 and Rs. 50 (and upwards) per day, respectively. In the case of certain operations like paddy harvesting, plucking of chillies and cutting of greengram, the wages were paid in accordance with very well established practices and conventions. For instance, for every four measures of chillies plucked one measure was given as wage to the labourer (during the peak time, the wage ratio became 3:1). The children did not participate in the activity contract because the ability of a child to contribute an equal part in the completion of the work was less. This became a contentious issue when wages had to be equally distributed with adults not taking children objecting to such an equal distribution. The ryots also objected to children's participation in activity contracts for certain operations (such as transplantation of paddy as the survival rate of transplantation done by children was perceived to be less, and thus, causing a loss to ryots).

The operations such as weeding, plucking of cotton and chillies were entrusted to *mutah* on the basis of a daily wage of Rs. 20 (Rs.25 when the demand was more) per day for a female agricultural labourer. The daily contract operations required very close supervision both from *maestri* and ryots. The working hours were normally 6 hours. The labourers were in the field on time, and liked to come back even before the time. Hence, the *maestri* went to each labourer's house in the morning to ensure that they reached the field on time and supplied water and other beverages to ensure that the labourers did not often break. Even if they had a break, it was ensured that it was not a very long break. Another contentious issue relating to daily contract was the preference of the labourers to take their children. The ryots did not like this as the children lagged in their work, and hence, their mothers completed the work of children. According to ryots, while two full wages were paid to mother and child, the work done was essentially equivalent to that of one-and-half persons.

Wages were normally to be paid at the end of the day (especially in the case of kind payments and/or after the completion of work. But the discussions with the labourers and *maestris* reveal that the wage payment was delayed 3-4 days in most of the cases, and by a fortnight in rare cases. This was because of the following reasons. First, some of the employers were small farmers and their finances were tight especially before they sold their produce. Second, the ryots might like to ascertain the work done before the payment was made. Third, the ryots might delay the payment if the work done was of inferior quality and/or children were taken for the work. They threatened that they would reduce the payment. The role of *maestri* was crucial in resolving the conflict. If participation of the children was an issue and the ryot was very rich and powerful, she made a moral argument in terms of poverty of the labourers and tried to convince him. If the ryot was meek, she bombarded him and threatened that the *mutah* would not work for him again. But, the cases of ryot not making payments were very rare[8] and the *maestri* somehow managed to resolve the conflict in such a way that the interests of the labourers were protected.

The wage distribution among labourers at their doorsteps was done soon after receiving the payment from the ryot. The *maestris* had accounts in their mind if the number of labourers was small around 20; if the number was large, they maintained an account (either on their own or with the help of a relative). In cases of delayed payments from ryots, the *maestri* made an advance from her own pocket or made an arrangement for labourers to procure provisions from a local grocery store.

During the slack season, the *mutah* labourers maximised the existing employment opportunities. A *mutah* consisting of 20 labourers undertook daily contract work of only 15 labourers, and all the labourers shared the wages. In some cases, the labourers migrated to eastern part of the district. The *maestri* would not recruit labourers from other *mutahs* during the slack season, as this would upset the more permanent members, and might result in them leaving the group.

The membership in a *mutah* was fairly stable over the years except that married girls went out of the group, while the newly wedded into the village came in. A labourer might have to leave the *mutah* when: (i) there was a delay in the distribution of wages by *maestri;* (ii) the *maestri* did not support her in taking children for daily contract; (iii) sufficient employment was not secured by the *mutah*; and (iv) when a relative of her own started a new *mutah*.

The *maestri* did not work along with labourers. She divided her work day among various activities relating to the management of *mutah* such as finding the work, collection of wages, conflict resolution, assignment of the work to the group, supervision and monitoring. In general, a *maestri* spent most of the time for the first three activities. Negotiating the work and remuneration, and collecting wages from ryots had become a challenging task because of the following factors:

- First, the tendencies of each of the actors to outsmart the other. The ryots liked to give an impression that the work involved for the *mutah* was less, and hence the remuneration should also be less. In contrast, the *maestri* and labourers would like to give an exactly opposite impression to the ryot while negotiating the remuneration. In order to do that, the *maestri* went around the fields of prospective clients to make a rough assessment of the quantum of work involved, and the remuneration that she should ask for. After a discussion within the *mutah* (normally lunch time in the field was utilised for this), she started the bargaining process with the ryots. At this stage, all the terms and conditions relating to quality of work and non-participation of children were to be accepted.

- Second, as stated by one of the *maestris*, the labourers had become very conscious of work timings. In the daily contract, they would not remain in the field the moment time was up. According to another *maestri*, earlier, more work, less wages was the practice. Now-a-days, labourers like to do less work for more wages. This attitude came in conflict with ryots' expectation on this quality of the work. Hence, the *maestri* had to ensure that the labourers maintained their timings and did quality work. Whenever the quality was not good the *maestri* had to put in her own labour.
- Third, the labourers brought their children even if the *maestri* had given a word that they would not be there in the field. If the ryots happened to notice that, the *maestri* covered it up with her own tactics; if she failed, parents and *maestri* helped the children to complete their work.
- Fourth, because the ryots and labourers had conflicting interests, obtaining a wage bill became difficult. The *maestri* had to make repeated visits (at times, spending much amount on transportation) to ryots to obtain the wage bill.

The income to the *maestri* varied across the groups, and was higher than that of an ordinary labourer. Under the daily contract, the ryot had to pay daily wage to her. If the *maestri* had sent two groups of labourers to two different ryots, she got two wages on that day. Under the activity contract, the *maestri* had this right for equal share of income. If the work done was of good quality and she managed to send labourers as per the requirement of the ryots, she got a bonus. In kind payments, she got a lion's share. According to one *maestri*, his/her income would be double of the ordinary labourer during the peak season, while it was 50 per cent more than what a labourer earned during the slack season. The labourers who were interviewed were all aware of additional payment to the *maestri*.

Performance of *Mutah* Labour

Almost all the labourers that were interviewed reported that employment opportunities and wages had gone up after joining the group. To the question of how the *mutah* was helpful to labourers, nearly half of them stated that the *mutah* provided them regular work and that too, at the doorstep. A significant proportion of them stated that more wage income earned (and kind wages) helped them in maintaining the family. The detailed discussions with *maestris* and labourers reveal the following:

(i) the maximisation of income and employment. Because of children's participation in the labour market and foot-dragging tactics, the labourers were able to earn more wage income for the family. By overworking during the peak season, they were able to maximise the employment opportunities during the peak season, and *mutah* helped them in getting work for the labourers for most part of the slack season;

(ii) the labourers did not spend their time and money in visiting the houses of ryots for work and receiving wages;

(iii) the (ii) above helped female agricultural labourers to spare more time for domestic chores and leisure;

(iv) under the activity contract, it was possible for female agricultural labourers to undertake those activities which were traditionally in the male domain, and earn more income; and

(v) the *mutah* labour helped in reducing the gender gap in wages especially during the peak season.

That the *mutah* helped the labourers could be found out from the pattern of asset acquisition by labourers in the selected villages. The proportion of labourers not acquiring any asset either before or after joining the *mutah* was nearly 50 per cent in Kothapeta and S. Amaravaram, while it was 14 per cent in Bathinapadu. Thus, a large proportion of the labourers had acquired both productive and consumption assets after joining in the *mutah* (Table 7.5). In some cases, land was bought, bullocks and buffaloes were acquired, and bicycles and auto-rickshaw were purchased to undertake income-generating activities. In some cases, gold was bought for personal security. In other cases, luxury goods such as television and fans were acquired. The *mutah* labour played an important role in the acquisition of assets. Each of the ALHs earned an income of Rs. 5,000 during the peak season and met the consumption needs relating to clothing, bulk purchase of rice, etc. This reduced their dependence on moneylenders. Added to that, there were well functioning self-help groups in micro-finance initiated by a local NGO, which provided them an opportunity to save and borrow out of their savings. Some of the ALHs were now in a position to lease in land. Although the ALHs experienced a shortfall in income during the slack season and the summer, the past savings, migration to eastern part of the district and self-help groups came to their rescue.

Table 7.5 : Acquisition of assets by labourers before and after joining the groups

Particulars	Bathinapadu		Kothapeta		S. Amaravaram	
	Before	After	Before	After	Before	After
House	4	3	1	3	1	
Land	1	2	3	2	1	2
Television		3		1		
Gold		1		2	1	2
Bicycle				1		2
Buffaloes		1	1	1	1	2
Bullocks		1	1			
Radio						
Fan		1		1		
Tape recorders				1		
Auto-rickshaw				1		
Not acquired		2		9		10

The *mutah* labour contributed to minimise the uncertainties of labour market, and improved the bargaining capacity of the labourers. According to one ryot, 'the *mutahs* frighten the ryots by saying that they will not come for the work if more wages are not paid'. According to another ryot, 'the *maestris* create lot of competition between the ryots and increase the demand for the labourers. This results in an increase of wages'. One ryot remarked the 'he is helpless with *maestri's* tactics'. These statements imply that 'the bargaining strength of labourers has improved, and this has resulted in obtaining more employment and wages for labourers'.

How is the *mutah* practice helpful to *maestris*? The widespread perception is that *maestris* earned income without doing much work, and some of them had prospered in the recent past. The socio-economic background of the *maestris* was the same as that of labourers; all of them belong to SC community, and a majority were landless and a few were marginal farmers. A comparison of landholding pattern between *maestris* and labourers shows that *maestris* were in fact worse off in terms of land ownership. In terms of acquisition of assets after the formation of *mutahs*, the *maestris*, however, scored over the labourers. But, both the labourers and ryots were appreciative of the role of *maestris* and sympathetic to their problems.

How is the *mutah* labour helpful to ryots? Over 35 per cent of the labourers stated that they got their work done quickly and properly, while one-fifth of them stated that they did not go in search of labourers to different houses. Flexibility in the mode of payment (cash or kind) was another perceived advantage to the ryots. A few labourers stated that they could get their work done without paying wages immediately. The *maestris* also held similar opinion on the utility of *mutah* labour to the ryots. But, the ryots themselves felt that the wage bill had gone up, and that whether the *mutah* was advantageous or not depended on the crops and the prices at which the produce was sold. They, however, acknowledged the benefits such as getting work done quickly, delayed payment and reduced supervision costs.

How is the *mutah* labour harmful to the *maestris*, ryots and labourers? An overwhelming majority of the labourers felt that the *mutah* labour was not at all harmful to the *maestris*. A few of them, however, noted that if the labourers did not do quality work, the *maestris* would face trouble from the ryots. A few of the *maestris* stated that they incurred loss of money if the ryots reduced the payment on account of poor quality of work and in transportation as they had to visit the ryots for a number of times.

As far as the ryots were concerned, more than 57 per cent of the labourers stated that the *mutah* was not harmful to them. About 13 per cent stated that children and old aged working in the fields were a loss to them. Labourers also perceived that work delays causing crop loss and difficult supervision were disadvantageous to the ryots. A small proportion of labourers also stated that the tendency of 'more people doing the work and dragging the things' was causing loss to the ryots.

How is the *mutah* harmful to labourers? Nearly 52 per cent of the labourers felt that it was not harmful to them. A few of them had, however, expressed that: (i) maintaining punctuality required in a *mutah* was difficult (especially when they had to complete domestic chores); (ii) working with *mutah* especially under activity contract was difficult; and (iii) irregular wage payments by the *maestris* put them in stress. About 15 per cent of the labourers stated that the *mutah* labour had a limitation in the sense that it had not solved the problem of unemployment in the slack season and in the summer season.

Conclusions

The last perceived limitation of *mutah* labour that it has not solved the problem of unemployment altogether is very important in making concluding remarks on the performance of *mutah* labour as an organising practice of the agricultural labourers.

The *mutah* labour is an effective collective strategy of agricultural labourers in securing more employment and wages, maximising the family income by recruiting children and the old aged, reducing the gender gap in wages, female workers undertaking those activities which are traditionally supposed to be done by men and in improving the bargaining power of the labourers. All these are well known infirmities of the agricultural labour market in India. The strong point of *mutah* labour is that it has succeeded in having a positive impact on these infirmities.

These benefits have, at best, solved the livelihood problems of the poor. The *mutah* labour scores less points when it comes to resources, knowledge and rights of the labourers. The agricultural labourers have acquired productive resources such as land, buffaloes, bullocks, etc. But, the proportion acquiring them is about 50 per cent in two villages. The knowledge levels among the agricultural labourers are very low. Very few are aware of the minimum wages. In most of the cases, girls are married at a very early age and the sample female agricultural labourers are not aware of legal age at which girls are to be married. The practice of recruiting children at very early age has its own implications for future poverty. As far as rights are concerned the *mutah* labour scores even less points. The *mutah* labourers are having more employment and wages because they perceive that they are able to exploit the situations of excess demand for labourers and inability of the ryots to closely supervise agricultural operations. They do not perceive that it is their right to get employment and minimum wages. They are not aware of the fact that legally different wages cannot be paid to men and women for the same operation. They do not perceive that children have right to their childhood and education.

One of the reasons why the *mutah* scores less points in resources, knowledge and rights is that the *mutahs* are not horizontally and vertically integrated into the decision-making and implementation channels. Once, a formal labour union invited the *mutahs* in the selected villages to join in a rally organised in Vijayawada City wherein the union advised them to go on strike for higher wages. In one of the villages, this was done; but, the ryots did not relent and the labourers had to work for the unchanged wages. The contact with the labour union was not revived further. Other organisations in the locality such as government departments, banks and NGOs are very well aware of *mutahs*; but, do not realise their potential in sustained poverty reduction. Hence, *mutahs* are kept outside their policies and programme implementation.

To conclude, the *mutah* labour, as an organising practice of the agricultural labourers, has succeeded in meeting the livelihood needs of the labourers. However, it did not significantly contribute to enhance the resources of the labourers, improve their knowledge and assert their rights. In other words, the *mutah* labour may have succeeded in poverty alleviation, but, the potentiality of *mutah* labour in poverty reduction is not realised and exploited either by labourers or local organisations who claim to be working on their behalf.

Notes

1. The proportion of casual labour to the total wage labour increased from 64.8 per cent in 1972-73 to 75.8 per cent in 1987-88.
2. Non-farm activities include small manufacturing, trades and services in

rural areas. Seasonal and contractual jobs unconnected with agriculture also fall under non-farm activities.

3. *Mutah* (a Telugu word) means that a closely-knit group, which takes care of its own interest.
4. *Maestri* is the one who organises, obtains, distributes and supervises the agricultural work and the principal spokesperson of a *mutah*
5. There has been 30 to 40 times increase in the value of land in the last three decades.
6. The land lease rates, which were low about 30 years ago, registered a sharp rise. The terms and conditions relating to land lease also changed over time. For instance, about 30 years ago, the rent could be paid after the harvest. About 15 years ago, half of the amount was to be paid before sowing. Nowadays, full amount of Rs. 4,000 per acre has to be paid before sowing. Raising this amount is difficult for the cultivators.
7. Only male *mutahs* function in quarrying, transportation of sand, etc.
8. We have come across only one case where the ryot reduced the agreed amount because the quality of the work was poor.

8

Conclusions

The emergence of NGOs as development actors in India implies that one can hope for more attention to the needs and concerns of the poor in policy formulation and implementation. This raises a number of questions. What has been the experience of NGOs in generating and facilitating the possibilities for the poor to exert influence on political and economic processes? How are their intervention strategies designed? Are the intervention strategies based on factors that historically generated poverty? Are they based on the condition and severity of poverty across different villages and different poverty groups within a village? Have they succeeded in enabling a political discourse in which poverty and poverty reduction are significant issues? Have they facilitated social and political practices among the poor so that decision-making, agendas, policy and programme implementation, etc., can be influenced at the local level?

It is in this context that the study aimed to :

(1) analyse the magnitude and severity of poverty and the processes generating poverty in the selected villages;
(2) examine the efforts made by the NGOs in alleviating poverty and to learn lessons in this regard;
(3) examine the efforts made by line departments, panchayat raj institutions at the village level and other agencies such as banks and credit cooperatives; and
(4) analyse the strategies adopted by the poor in coming out of poverty.

Summary and Conclusions

The chapter-wise summary and conclusions have been provided below:

Action Research Methods for Poverty Alleviation

One of the objectives of the study was to build the capacity of the NGO workers and target group in finding the situation and needs of the target group and prepare action plans in this regard. In order to achieve this objective extensive documentation on the process and outcomes on Action Research Project (ARP) was attempted.

The ARP provided valuable inputs to those organisations, which wanted to become learning ones. It also enabled the project initiators to understand the situation of the poor, their needs, and prepare an action plan to alleviate poverty based on situation and needs. For poverty reduction to take place, the process of learning, action, and reflection should become an integral part of an organisation. It was not sufficient if this was taken as a one-time project and follow-up was not adequate.

The PRA techniques were particularly helpful to enable people's participation. But, there were limitations such as longer time needed if the exercise was to be conducted in larger number of villages and difference between these methods and survey. The survey would capture the views of several people on what strategies needed to be adopted, while the same might not be possible in PRA exercises if effective facilitation was not done. Thus, there was trade-off between survey and PRA if the exercise was to be conducted in a larger number of villages. This could be sorted out by conducting social mapping, WRE, seasonality mapping and focus group interviews, and canvassing a short questionnaire on strategies and local organisations. The difference between the results of survey and PRA could be sorted out with the help of a daily review of the process.

There was a danger that the needs-analysis might result in coming up with a shopping list and that people might show preference to poverty alleviation rather than poverty reduction. It was also possible that the poor might come up with individual strategies aimed at their survival and security. They might not come up with the political strategies that would have influence on structures that perpetuated inequality and that generated poverty. Hence, this aspect needed to be borne in mind from the beginning.

For significant and sustainable impact on poverty reduction, situation analysis, needs assessment and preparation of action plan should become integral to the intervention process adopted by an organisation. Where this was difficult, there was a need to collaborate with Gram Panchayats, which were also supposed to prepare area plans based on the methodology outlined in this chapter. If these two actors could come together in this area of action research, the benefits to the community could be enormous.

Condition and Severity of Poverty in the Selected Villages

The PRA methods such as mapping the trends, social mapping, wealth ranking exercise, seasonality mapping, focus group interviews and extensive survey of literature were used to assess the condition and severity of poverty across the selected villages. The magnitude of poverty varied within and across the villages. In general, most of the poor households belonged to SC community. The severity of poverty also varied; in general, it was among SC households. Even among these households, the women bore the brunt of poverty. The principal causes of poverty were lack of endowment (lack of assets such as land) and exchange failures (unemployment) and these were cited as important reasons. The historical analysis shows that commercialisation of agriculture mainly contributed to widespread poverty.

Poverty Alleviation Interventions by NGOs

An analysis of poverty alleviation interventions by NGOs reveals that the main programmes undertaken by them were related to starting economic programmes and micro-finance to enable the poor to access credit for income generation and also use the strength of the organisation (namely, SHGs) to obtain political and social empowerment. The results of the analysis are as follows:

The craft activity started by SHARE was successful in so far as enabling women members to obtain employment and earning incomes. Although incomes tended to be small and uncertain, they were valued by women members. Skills relating to craft activity were acquired and thereby, improving the confidence in members. Craft centre provided women an opportunity to come together everyday and discuss their personal problems. In the process, awareness and knowledge on government programmes and gram panchayats were acquired.

SHGs were started to cover a larger proportion of poor and to provide a forum for women to come together. Since they were formed only two years ago, it is too early to assess their role in poverty alleviation and empowerment. But, the indications are that there is cohesiveness within the groups, leadership is emerging and groups are being managed by members themselves. Savings are contributed regularly, and this amount provides confidence and security to women. As of now, women mainly borrow for consumption and crop production. Not much credit is provided to initiate income generation activities. Further, not many women are coming forward to borrow for income generation as they face constraints (lack of skills and capital, inability to find an activity that can fetch them income higher than that available in wage labour, segmented non-farm labour market, societal constraints, etc.).

Another conclusion based on the evidence on the proportion of women's income to total income was that women's income formed a large proportion of the total income. A majority of such households were headed by women and the contribution of male income was low (often due to illness, drinking). The evidence also suggests that enabling women to earn income might result in a situation of male members withdrawing from the labour market. This phenomenon put a lot of pressure on them. We are not suggesting that women should not be provided with opportunities to earn income; what we are suggesting is that men should also be brought within the purview of development intervention if women are to be empowered.

Although SHARE initiated development activities with all sincerity to empower women through income generation activities, we do not find much evidence to suggest non-economic benefits are taking place. This suggests that economic programmes need not necessarily be a good strategy for women's empowerment. There are larger societal and political forces that constrain women to have empowerment especially in non-economic fields. We suggest that different types of interventions (not entirely based on economic programmes) are to be initiated, if poverty reduction is to take place.

An analysis of the economic benefits of micro-finance programmes on members of SHGs in the project area of Sanghamitra revealed that the condition of households in the member group was better than those in the comparison group in the following respects:

- The households in the member group had access to credit facility.
- The households in the member group were different from those in the comparison group in terms of total amount saved and number of savings forms used.
- As far as acquisition of productive assets was concerned, a relatively larger proportion of households from the member group had acquired assets such as livestock and land as compared to those in the comparison group.
- Most of the households in the member group had access to more than two livelihood sources as compared to those in the comparison group.
- Most of the households in the member group obtained more than Rs. 20,000 of income in a year. On the other hand, a relatively larger proportion of the households from the comparison group obtained less than Rs. 20,000 of annual income.
- The higher income in the case of member households had a favourable impact on the acquisition of consumer durables and expenditure on food, education and health.
- While there were significant economic benefits on members of micro-finance groups, the social benefits seemed to be marginal. The decision-making was mostly confined to small and large purchases for the household, self and children. A majority of the women, even after years of membership in the group, did not participate in the decision-making relating to house repair, purchase of land, productive assets, education of boys and girls, etc., as these areas were considered to be the domains of men in the household.

The educational levels of the household members in the case of member group were substantially better than those in the comparison group. However, a significant proportion of women from both the groups stated that girls should be married soon after they attained puberty. Most of the women from both member and comparison groups stated that they would give unlimited freedom for boys to pursue their education. It, therefore, appears that the societal expectations on the age at which girls are to be married and whether women can undertake salaried employment determined the parental decision on whether the girl should go to school or not. This is a very well known position and is applicable to women belonging to the member group as well. The obvious conclusion is that the SHG membership has not made any significant difference to the value attached to children's education (especially girls). The observed differences in school attendance between member and comparison groups are to be, therefore, attributed to factors other than the micro-finance.

Years of membership in micro-finance groups has made only marginal difference in so far as the participation of women in the political institutions, and their awareness on who were important political leaders at the time of the survey. In this respect, the women in the comparison group from the project area of Sanghamitra were relatively better. But, it is not clear to what extent this could be attributed to generally higher levels of awareness in Krishna district or to micro-finance groups. The qualitative evidence on participation in political institutions indicates that the SHG membership had not really contributed to gaining awareness on rights that the women had and how to utilize these rights.

Poverty Alleviation Interventions by Local Organisations

The data base for an analysis of poverty alleviation interventions by local organisations other than NGOs was organisational mapping and interviews with the concerned officials and political leaders. An important conclusion from this analysis is as follows. The main causes of poverty, according to people, were lack of assets (land) and unemployment. The poverty alleviation programmes that were being carried out by the local organisations had the potential to address these problems. But, the evidence points out that the programmes were mainly related to PDS, OAP and some bank loans. These did not address the main causes of poverty. Further, banks did not provide credit for income generation or asset building. The programmes of gram panchayat were essentially related to building the infrastructure in the village, and they did not incorporate the concerns of the peo Thus, there was no clear congruence between the situation of the poor and poverty alleviation programmes undertaken by the local organisations.

Poverty Alleviation Strategies of the People

One of the important strategies adopted by the people in Andhra villages was to organise themselves as gang labour. An analysis was carried out with the help of data collected from labourers, farmers and leaders of *mutah* labour groups. The *mutah* labour improved the bargaining position of the labourers. However, a few of the labourers stated that the *mutah* labour had a limitation in the sense that it had not solved the problem of unemployment in the slack season and in the summer season. This is very important in making concluding remarks on the performance of *mutah* labour as an organising practice of the agricultural labourers.

The *mutah* labour is an effective collective strategy of agricultural labourers in securing more employment and wages, maximising the family income by recruiting children and the old aged, reducing the gender gap in wages, female workers undertaking those activities which are traditionally supposed to be done by men and in improving the bargaining power of labourers. All these are well known infirmities of the agricultural labour market in India. The strong point of *mutah* labour is that it has succeeded in having a positive impact on these infirmities.

These benefits have, at best, solved the livelihood problems of the poor. The *mutah* labour scores less points when it comes to resources, knowledge and rights of the labourers. The agricultural labourers have acquired productive resources such as land, buffaloes, bullocks, etc. But, the proportion acquiring them is about 50 per cent in two villages. The knowledge levels among the agricultural labourers are very low. Very few are aware of minimum wages. In most of the cases, girls are married at very early age and the sample female agricultural labourers are not aware of legal age at which girls are to be married. The practice of recruiting children at very early age has its own implications for future poor and poverty. As far as the rights are concerned the *mutah* labour scores even less points. The *mutah* labourers are having more employment and wages because they perceive that they are able to exploit the situations of excess demand for labourers and inability of ryots to closely supervise agricultural operations. They do not perceive that it is their right to get employment and minimum wages. They are not aware of the fact that legally different wages cannot be paid to men and women for the same operation. They do not perceive that children have the right to their childhood and education.

One of the reasons why *mutah* scores less points in resources, knowledge and rights is that the *mutahs* are not horizontally and vertically integrated into the decision-making and implementation channels. Once, a formal labour union invited the *mutahs* in the selected villages to join in a rally organised in Vijayawada City wherein the union advised them to go on strike for higher wages. In one of the villages, this was done; but, the ryots did not relent and the labourers had to work for the unchanged wages. The contact with the labour union was not revived further. Other organisations in the locality such as government departments, banks and NGOs are very well aware of *mutahs*; but, do not realise their potential in sustained poverty reduction. Hence, *mutahs* are kept outside their policies and programme implementation.

Thus, the *mutah* labour, as an organising practice of the agricultural labourers, has succeeded in meeting the livelihood needs of the labourers. However, it did not significantly contribute to enhance the resources of the labourers, improve their knowledge and assert their rights. In other words, the *mutah* labour may have succeeded in poverty alleviation. But, the potentiality of *mutah* labour in poverty reduction is not realised and exploited either by labourers or local organisations who claim to be working on their behalf.

To conclude, the important causes of poverty were lack of assets and unemployment. The local organisations formed for them have had only limited in addressing these causes. The NGOs which are supposed to have facilitated the mechanisms to enable the poor to represent their interests and secure them have also had limited success in this regard for the following reasons :

In the organisational mapping conducted in Tamil Nadu villages, the people rated PDS, protected water supply (through panchayat) and schools (where noon-meal is provided) as the most important local organisations contributing to their poverty alleviation. The next important organisation was SHARE. Banks and cooperatives came in the distant fifth. Gram panchayat and line departments came last;

on the map, they were shown as organisations which were located very, very far. The pattern was similar in the village where the NGO is working except that SHARE was not in the picture. This suggests that the presence of a NGO does not make any difference to the functioning of local organisations notwithstanding that it had facilitated the formation of institutional channels for the poor to represent their interests in the other local organisations. What are the contributing factors?

First, the basis for the intervention strategy of NGOs was not entirely rooted in the poverty condition and processes in the local area. The historical analysis on processes generating poverty the Tamil Nadu villages showed that new agricultural technology and lift irrigation together with cropping pattern changes resulted in widespread unemployment and uncertain livelihood for the poor. One might have expected that, given this context, the NGO had initiated work relating to representing the interests of the poor in the local labour market and securing their rights relating to employment and wages. Instead, the organisation began with income generation activity. One may argue that this will also address the problem of unemployment. But, as the discussion on condition of poverty showed, the unemployment continues to be an important problem of the poor even after nearly 14 years of work by SHARE in employment and income generation.

Secondly, even if the NGOs wanted to represent the interests of the poor in the labour market, one wonders whether this would have been possible. This was because, as the discussion on historical changes in the socio-economic status of the different sections showed, some of the SC households became well-off largely because of individual and entrepreneur based strategies. This suggests that, historically, it was not the socio-political process among the poor which helped them to influence decision-making, agendas, policy and programme implementation at the local level. Largely, it was individual efforts which helped some households to become better-off. The discussions with poorest and poor households also reveal that they preferred individual strategies to come out of their poverty. This further implies that the collective memory of the poor was not one of social and political processes where they had influenced the policy and implementation issues in their favour[1]; but, something else. This was not conducive for the NGOs to enable the poor in poverty reduction.

Thirdly, the institutional channels that the NGOs created are to be examined whether they help the poor to access, control and contest the policy formulation and implementation. The SHGs formed are not homogeneous, and consisted of poorest, poor and others. In one of the SHGs, a woman belonging to the well-off category managed to join in the group, and even functioned as its leader until recently. When asked about the poverty alleviation strategies that the poor should follow, she noted that individual strategies were the best. When asked about collective struggles to secure the rights of the poor in the labour market, she stated that she was not in favour of them as the reason for being poor was not due to low wages, but because of laziness. While not getting into the temptation of generalisation on the basis of this case, it can be suggested that the heterogeneity may come in the way of generating and facilitating the possibilities for the poor to exert influence on political and economic process.

As the discussion on condition and severity of poverty reveals that poverty is complex and the nature of poverty differs across the villages and caste groups within a village. In such a situation, one wonders whether the formation of institutional channel like SHGs and craft centres with almost identical functions and activities will help the poor to access and contest the policy formulation and implementation.

The institutional channels created by the NGO are also not utilised in the way that would help the poor to have opportunities for poverty reduction. Regarding the question on what was discussed in the meetings of the craft centre and SHGs, one woman from Tamil Nadu villages stated that 'we discuss personal problems'. Another women gave an example of an issue relating to domestic violence which was discussed in the craft centre. The discussion with this woman member suggested that the other members counselled her to be patient, and things would sort out on their own. But, a significant proportion of the members stated that they were preoccupied with the production of palm-leaf products; so much so that they only talked about orders, production, quality and meeting deadlines. The monthly meetings of SHGs were mainly utilised for savings collection and to arrive at lending decisions. Very little time was spent on discussing issues relating to the community and to their poverty. For instance, although the mandatory gram sabha meetings were not held in the last two years, women members had not discussed this issue, let alone pressing the gram panchayat to hold one such meeting.

The institutional channels also seemed to be inadequate for the purpose of providing opportunities for the poor to influence political processes. For instance, there was no forum either at the village level and at the level of gram panchayat where members of SHGs and craft centres could come together to exert influence on political and economic processes. Similarly, there was no federation of SHGs at the project level.

SHARE is part of only one NGO network which helps the organisation to market its products in the international market. Although it makes efforts to enable the poor to access the resources from the government and banks by empowering them, the main strategy used is to mobilise the resources for its target group on its own. The organisation believes that it can achieve success in resource mobilisation because of: (i) the image that SHARE is sincere, transparent, democratic and accountable organisation; (ii) the networks that the organisation was built with the officials and bankers in the district; and (iii) representative status accorded to some of the office bearers of SHARE in the district decision-making committees. So far, the priority given to building or becoming part of NGO networks to represent the interests of the poor in the policy formulation and implementation is low. Sanghamitra has been part of NGO network in the district; this has helped the NGO to represent the interest of the poor to some extent.

Fourthly, the existence of poverty at the local level is recognised and causes of poverty are identified by the poor themselves. The political discourse on poverty at the local level probably stops here. The views on culpability for the condition of the poor and the emphasis on individual strategies suggest that the political discourse on poverty at the local level remains very broad and diffused. And that, very often, the discussion on who is responsible for poverty alleviation does not take place at the local level. It is not very surprising, therefore, that the target group members of NGOs do not discuss about the 'non-conduct of gram sabha meetings'. This is because of the widespread perception that the mandate given to gram panchayats is not poverty reduction; but, something else. Both banks and decentralised government can do a lot for poverty reduction. While banks and line departments do not work, the decentralised government does not address the important causes of poverty. The work relating to sanitation, protected water supply and road construction is all important for poverty alleviation. But, though gram panchayats can take up work relating to the desilting of the tanks, improving the water table in the locality, providing sanitary facilities for women, undertaking employment oriented public works for the poor, etc., they do not seem to be on the agenda. The target group does not make any efforts to take the discourse on poverty to the local organisations as they are unsure about who is responsible for their poverty reduction.

Fifthly, the target group members of NGOs also cannot count on the support of other poor in the villages because of exclusive practices adopted. For instance, in one of the meetings on organisational mapping, there was a difference of opinion on the placement of SHARE. Two of its members wanted to give higher rating to SHARE on the grounds that the craft centre provided employment for almost all the year, SHGs provided loans to those who could not access them from banks, provide supplementary education to children and training on a wide ranging issues to women. Others present agreed with the reasoning; but, rejected the rating. Their argument was that these positive things happen in the case of only SHARE members, who numbered only around 20-25 in the village. Since the number of poor was much more than this, a higher rating could not be assigned to SHARE. This suggests that SHARE's work in income generation and welfare may have helped its own target group; but, it has failed to include the other poor to join in the endeavour to represent the interests of the poor in the policy formulation and implementation.

Notwithstanding that the objective of NGOs is empowerment of poor women and they have been making sincere efforts to achieve this objective by implementing programmes and activities aimed at livelihood provision and capacity building, they have been facing constraints and obstacles in generating the possibilities for the poor to reduce their poverty. The constraints are deficiencies in its technical and political capacity. The obstacles are wider socio-economic and political processes and lack of pro-poor attitude among the other local organisations. Given that NGOs alone cannot reduce poverty and other local organisations are deficient in redressing the problems of the poor, poverty reduction remains to be an outstanding problem, and calls for linkages among local organization for sustained alleviation of poverty.

Note

1. The *dalit* movement that was referred to earlier mainly concentrated on improving the dignity of the *dalits*. The struggles were mainly against untouchability and restrictions on temple entry.

Bibliography

Andersen, Per Pinstrup and Mauricio Jaramillo (1993). The Impact of Technological Change on Food Consumption and Nutrition. In Peter B.R. Hazell and C. Ramasamy (eds.), *The Green Revolution Reconsidered: The Impact of High Yielding Rice Varieties in South India.* New Delhi: Oxford University Press.

Aziz, Abdul (1993). *Decentralised Planning: The Karnataka Experiment.* New Delhi: Sage.

Bandara, C.M. Madduma (1977). Hydrological Consequences of Agrarian Change. In B.H. Farmer (ed.), *Green Revolution.* London: Macmillan.

Baulch (1996). Neglected Trade offs in Poverty Measurement. *IDS Bulletin,* 27(1) : 36-42.

Bhalla, Sheila (1993), The Dynamics of Wage Determination and Employment Generation in Indian Agriculture. *Indian Journal of Agricultural Economics*, 48(3) : 448-70.

Bhalla, Surjit (2002). Growth and Poverty in India: Myth and Reality. In M. Govinda Rao (ed.), *Development, Poverty and Fiscal Policy: Decentralization of Institutions.* New Delhi: Oxford University Press.

Chambers, Robert (1988). Poverty in India: Concepts, Research and Reality. *Discussion Paper 241.* Brighton: IDS.

Chambers, Robert (1995). Poverty and Livelihoods: Whose Reality Counts? *Discussion Paper 347.* Brighton: IDS.

Chinnappa, B.N. (1977). Adoption of the New Technology in North Arcot District. In B.H. Farmer (ed.), *Green Revolution?* London: Macmillan.

Datt, G. (1997). *Poverty in India and Indian States: An Update.* Washington: International Food Policy Research Institute.

Datt, Gaurav (1996), *Bargaining Power, Wages and Employment: An Analysis of Agricultural Labour Markets in India.* New Delhi: Sage.

Dev, S. Mahendra (2002). Poverty in India: Trends, Macro Policies and Direct Programmes. In M. Govinda Rao (ed.), *Development, Poverty and Fiscal Policy: Decentralization of Institutions.* New Delhi: Oxford University Press.

Dreze, J. and A. Sen (1989). *Hunger and Public Action.* Oxford: Clarendon Press.

Duvvury, Nata (1999). Imperialism and the Social Framework of Commercialisation of Agriculture in Dry-Land South India: A Study of Tobacco in Guntur District. In G.N. Rao and D. Rajasekhar (eds.), *The Economy and Society in Colonial Andhra* (forthcoming).

Edwards, Michael and David Hulme (1996). Too Close for Comfort? The Impact of Official Aid on Non-Governmental Organisations. *World Development,* 24 (6) : 451-73.

Edwards, Michael and David Hulme (eds.) (1995). *Non-Governmental Organisations — Performance and Accountability: Beyond the Magic Bullet.* London: Earthscan.

Farmer, B.H. (ed.) (1977). *Green Revolution?* London: Macmillan.

Gopalan, Sarala (2002). *Towards Equality — The Unfinished Agenda – Status of Women in India (2001),* New Delhi: National Commission for Women.

Harris, B. (1977). Rural Electrification and the Diffusion of Electric Water-lifting Technology in North Arcot District, India. In B.H. Farmer, (ed.) *Green Revolution?* London: Macmillan.

Harris, J. (1977). The Limitations of HYV Technology in North Arcot District: the View from a Village. In B.H. Farmer, (ed.), *Green Revolution?* London: Macmillan.

Harris, J. (1993). The Green Revolution in North Arcot: Economic

Trends, Household Mobility and the Politics of an "Awkward Class". In Peter B.R. Hazell, and C. Ramasamy (eds.), *The Green Revolution Reconsidered: The Impact of High Yielding Rice Varieties in South India.* New Delhi: Oxford University Press.

Harris-White, Barbara and S. Janakarajan, (1997). From Green Revolution to Rural Industrial Revolution in South India. *Economic and Political Weekly.* XXXII (25) : 1469-77.

Hazell, Peter. B.R. and C. Ramasamy (eds.) (1993). *The Green Revolution Reconsidered: The Impact of High Yielding Rice Varieties in South India.* New Delhi: Oxford University Press.

Janakarajan, S. (1996). Ecological Crisis and Agrarian Distress? The Tale of Irrigation Development in Northern Tamil Nadu. A Paper Presented at the *Workshop on Adjustment and Development: Agrarian Change, Markets and Social Welfare,* Madras: Chennai Institute of Development Studies.

Joshi, S., *et. al* (1997). *Experience of Advocacy in Environment and Development.* Bangalore: DSI and NOVIB.

Kabeer, Naila (1996). Agency, Well-Being and Inequality: Reflections on Gender Dimensions of Poverty. *IDS Bulletin,* 27 (1) : 11-21.

Kannan, K.P. (1993). Labour Institutions and Economic Development in India – Some Exploratory Analysis. *Indian Journal of Labour Economics,* 37(1).

Murthy, R.K. and Nitya Rao (1998). *Indian NGOs, Poverty Alleviation and Their Capacity Enhancement in the 1990s: An Institutional and Social Relations Perspective.* New Delhi: FES.

Murugesan, K. (1999). Experiences of "SHARE" in its Attempt at Ensuring Participation of Women in the Election to Local Administration. In D. Rajasekhar (ed.), *Decentralised Government and NGOs: Issues, Strategies and Ways Forward.* New Delhi: Concept.

Nair, C.V. (1991). Rural Credit: Emerging Issues and Challenges. In Surjit Singh (ed.), *Rural Credit: Issues for the Nineties.* New Delhi: Oxford and IBH.

Pedersen, Lars-Engberg and Neil Webster (1998). On Political Space: Locating the Workshop, A Paper Presented at the *Workshop on LORPA IV Gilbjerghoved, Gilelege,* Denmark, August 24-25.

PRIA (1991). *Voluntary Development Organisations in India: A Study of History, Roles and Future Challenges.* New Delhi: PRIA.

Rajakutty, S. (1997). Development of Women and Children in Rural Areas (DWCRA): Are We in the Right Course? *Journal of Rural Development,* 16 (1) : 85-112.

Rajamma, G. and V. C. Nadarajan (1997). *Mid-Term Review of SHARE's Activities.* Vellore: SHARE, mimeo.

Rajasekhar, D. (1998). Rural Development Strategies of NGOs. *Journal of Social and Economic Development*, 1(2) : 306-27.

Rajasekhar, D. (2000). Non-Governmental Organisations (NGOs): Opportunities and Challenges. *ISEC Working Paper 66.* Bangalore: ISEC.

Rajasekhar, D. and Namerta (1994). Wage Labour in the Agricultural Sector. In Sarath Davala (ed.), *Unprotected Labour in India: Issues and Concerns,* New Delhi: FES.

Rajasekhar, D. and Vinod Vyasulu, (1990). Rural Credit Delivery System: A Study in Pali District of Rajasthan, *Economic and Political Weekly,* XXV (39): A-125-A-134.

Rajasekhar, D. and Narasimha Reddy (1997). *Local Development Programmes and NGOs: A Guide on Local Government Programmes for Field-workers.* Bangalore: BCO and NOVIB.

Rao, G.N. (1985). Transition from Subsistence to Commercialised Agriculture: A Study of Krishna District of Andhra. *Economic and Political Weekly,* XX (25-6) : A-60-A-69.

Rao, G.N. and D. Rajasekhar (1991). Commodity Production and the Changing Agrarian Scenario in Andhra: A Study in Inter-Regional Variations, c. 1910 - c. 1947. In S. Bhattacharya, *et al.* (eds.), *South Indian Economy c.1914 -1947.* New Delhi: Oxford University Press.

Rao, K. Subba (1980). Institutional Credit, Uncertainty and Adoption of HY(V) Technology: A Comparison of East and West Uttar Pradesh. *Indian Journal of Agricultural Economics,* 40(1): 69-90.

Rath, N. (1985). 'Garibi Hatao': Can IRDP do it? *Economic and Political Weekly,* 20(6) : 238-406.

Reddy, Narasimha and D. Rajasekhar (1996). *Development Programmes and NGOs: A Guide on Central Government Programmes for NGOs in India.* Bangalore: BCO and NOVIB.

Robinson, M. (1993): Governance, Democracy and Conditionality: NGOs and the New Policy Agenda. In A Clayton (ed.) *Governance, Democracy and Conditionality: What Role for NGOs?* Oxford: INTRAC.

Rudra, A. (1982). *Indian Agricultural Economics: Myths and Realities*. New Delhi: Allied Publishers.

Saxena, N.C. (2000). How Have the Poor Done? Mid-term Review of Ninth Plan. *Economic and Political Weekly*, XXXV (41) : 3627-3[illegible].

Sen, A.K. (1981). *Poverty and Famines: An Essay on Entitlements*. New Delhi: Oxford University Press.

Sen, Abhijit (1996), Economic Reforms, Employment and Poverty: Trends and Options, *Economic and Political Weekly*, XXXI (35, 36 and 37) : 2459-77.

Stephen, F. (1990). *NGOs: Hope of the Last Decade of This Century*. Bangalore: SEARCH.

Swift, Jeremy (1989). Why are Rural People Vulnerable to Famines? *IDS Bulletin*, 20(2).

Tandon, P.K. (1988). A Note on Rural Indebtedness. *Social Scientist*, 16 (4).

Unni, Jeemol, (1991). Regional Variations in Rural Non-Agricultural Employ-ment: An Exploratory Analysis, *Economic and Political Weekly*, XXVI (3) : 109-22.

Vaidyanathan, A. (1987), Labour Use in Rural India: A Study of Spatial and Temporal Variations. *Economic and Political Weekly*, XX[illegible] (52) : A130-A 146.

Vaidyanathan, A. (1994). The Employment Situation: Some Emerging Perspectives', *Economic and Political Weekly,* XXIX (50) : 3147-56.

Webster, Neil and Lars Engberg Pedersen (2002). *In the Name of the Poor: Contesting Political Space for Poverty Reduction.* London: Zed.

World Bank (1996). *India: Five Years of Stabilisation and Reforms and Challenges Ahead.* Washington D.C.: The World Bank.

World Bank (2000), *Overview of Decentralization, a Draft,* Washington, D.C: The World Bank.

Index